SHEAR GIFTS

— • —

FINDING HOPE WHEN LIFE IS HARD

CHRISTY FOLDENAUER

ILLUMINE
MEDIA

— · —

GRATITUDE

To my family, Adam, Ashton, Lauren & Nate, who have been incredibly patient, loving, and encouraging in every step of this process

To J. Andrew Edwards at Engelhaven Editorial, for believing in this project, and for making me better, line by line

To Nicole, who listened to my highs and lows on this project, and who always has my back, truly, on my best and worst days

To my mother, who held up my arms in many moments, and exhorted me to bring this over the finish line

To Laura B., who was first to finish these pages as an early reader, and who was a buoy of hope when I needed it

To Anne, who generously shared her creative gifts to help me keep moving forward

To Chantal, Sarah, Brianna, and Katherine for sounding this out with me early on, and helping me keep this work applicable and real

To Janet and Steve for sharing their knowledge with me and helping me get this into the hands of many

To Mike, who made ChrisMike productions happen after decades of our mother planning it, and who guided me through the land of audio production

To the Institute for Contemporary Art at VCU, and their incredible Media Center team, who extended studio space and continuous support in the creation of the audio book format of this material

To Josh, Matt, Laura M., Sonya, Vernon, Van-Neisha, Cheryl, John, Irma and Paul for speaking truth into my life, and helping me to keep pushing forward at pivotal moments in the last two years

But mostly, gratitude to God, whom I believe initiated this content deep within my soul, to Jesus, whose example I'm constantly striving to follow, and to the Holy Spirit, who has undoubtedly kept me in step and on the path, equipping me at every turn on this journey of writing.

PREFACE

"God can get tiny, if we're not careful."
—Gregory Boyle

Sometimes in recent years, I have felt like Hope was playing hide-and-seek.

For the record, I'm lousy at that game; I'm too loud to hide well, too impatient to seek for more than a moment. But there's something I've learned that you should know right away: Hope has a way of finding you when you least expect it and revealing herself when you go looking with even a modicum of patience and perseverance.

So, this is a book about Hope: a Hope I found in unexpected places, and the Hope I found in *all* the expected places once I started to really seek. For once, I feel like the big winner at hide-and-seek. (Maybe this is some sort of last-shall-be-first redemption for my awkward childhood-game experiences, where I was often last-to-be-picked and first-to-be-out!).

For all my hardship on the playground at recess, the classroom is where I usually showed my prowess. Big ideas and vocabulary gems have always been my wheelhouse; that love has taken me through progressive roles in communication, human resources, sales leadership, marketing, and then, of all places, seminary. For seven years, I worked vocationally as a pastor.

I loved being a pastor, and yet, amid a pandemic, any semblance of balance in the role was all-too-elusive, so I stepped out of leading a local church and into the role of pastor-at-large. This book is the fruit of some of those early days, as I rediscovered my sense of call beyond the walls of a church, working out the angst of yielding something I loved deeply—and figuring out where Hope might be.

As it turned out, she was hiding in plain sight.

These pages are both deeply personal and, I believe, fully universal. If I didn't believe that they would bless others, I would have kept this as a journal and simply lingered in the ideas myself. (Believe me, that would have been easier!) But, at some point, my daily journal pages, colorful mind maps, and lectio divina became something I was compelled to share with others. I felt a nudge that I was tapping into something that others were also struggling with, and that's the day I started writing.

In addition to the work of writing, I have found a new home as an entrepreneur, bringing light to corporate spaces and helping executives and teams. I also continue to minister and preach, because, once-a-pastor, always-a-pastor. The ideas in this book have found their way in different forms into both spaces—spiritual and entrepreneurial—and have been met with a hunger that's kept me writing, playing with ideas, and bringing the metaphors and concepts into all the places I can.

Especially through my coaching work of late, I've realized that how we frame the experiences of life matters greatly. In this book, I hope to offer you a new frame. It's a frame I stumbled into as I kept showing up to daily Bible reading and prayer.

I've noticed that sometimes in Christian circles, we skirt over the harder parts of the story with Pollyanna phrases and don't point to God's goodness until the difficulty is done or the situation is resolved. By God's grace, let's outgrow that way of thinking. This book takes the opposite approach, because I believe God is present in profound ways in the most difficult of spaces. Even more, specifically *naming* that presence in our hearts and minds and out loud, to others, while we're still in the thick of it, enables us to keep moving forward and find that Hope we've been seeking.

The writing of this book has, for me, become a place of healing. I extend it to you, in hopes that the ideas might meet you in even a fraction of the way that they've worked wholeness in me.

So, here's my offer: let's stop counting down, and let's get out there and find Hope together. You might be surprised by how often she's hiding in plain sight.

Three, two, one—*"Ready or not, here we come!"*

I've organized these ideas into three parts. The first section speaks to the places we feel a disconnect spiritually, but we're not quite sure why. Jesus offers a brilliant analogy for this, and it relates to the soil of your heart. We'll look at how soil changes, and what to do if you find you're in a different place than you want to be. The second section addresses the times in life when we experience loss of something: how do we understand and respond to seasons of downsizing or losing, as it relates to our faith life? The final section is about times in spiritual life where we feel we are only holding steady and not contributing or producing as we have before. These times that feel unfruitful can be disorienting at a minimum and are both discouraging and disheartening for many Christians. How can we better understand where God is at work in times where we don't feel the same level of fruitfulness?

Maybe the most pressing question, if you're holding this book, is this: Is all of this—the spiritual disconnect I feel, the sense of deep loss, and the seeming inability to be fruitful—*permanent?* Is this my "new normal," spiritually speaking?

So let me answer that one right here, in order to offer you some hope as you begin. No, what you're experiencing is not what you'll *always* be feeling, because we serve a God who is constantly speaking and helping us to move forward. Many of us have picked up habits during the pandemic, however, that do not serve us well in our spiritual lives, and sorting those out is an important part of this process of returning to spiritual health.

One thing that helps us to make sense of the landscape we're in, so that we may move forward in our faith, is to name the explicit dynamics at work and learn how to move past them. That's what this book is about: providing some language for what we've all been through and some new ways to connect with God in this season of slow recuperation. As a fellow sojourner who is barely just a step or two ahead of you on this path, I promise you that God is here.

Throughout this work, you'll read Scripture in a translation called *The Message*, which was completed by Eugene Peterson and published in segments between 1993 and 2002. Peterson intentionally used many modern idioms, and his translation of Scripture is thought-for-thought, as opposed to word-for-word. It's important to know this as you approach *The Message*, because the translation feels quite different from other translations. Peterson strove to create a translation that would capture the modern reader, much in the same way that the original words would have captured the original reader.

The Message translation has been critical in my own spiritual formation over the past several years, as it has opened up passages that I had all but memorized in other translations. It has given me fresh language for ancient spiritual concepts, blessing me with ever new experiences of Scripture. In short, I'm not sure you'd be holding this book if it weren't for Eugene Peterson's work in translating *The Message*. His translation is what sparked many of the ideas in this book for me. Faithfulness builds on faithfulness, and I absolutely stand on Peterson's shoulders in this regard.

Finally, because spiritual life is closely connected to our emotional well-being, portions of this book will address aspects of emotional health, including thought patterns, feelings, and our response to them. Please remember as you read that I am a pastor, not a professional counselor or licensed therapist. While I've spent considerable time studying emotional well-being, I write as a fellow journeyer, not a clinician. Please don't receive this book as a substitute for the advice and care of a mental health professional. For the record, I recommend establishing a relationship with a great counselor; it is always a good idea to engage with a professional who can help you think through your emotional health and well-being.

**A Prayer to Remember the
Lord is Near**

Where there are broken
pieces,
shards and the sharpest
edges,
where you fear taking steps
amidst your fragmented
past,
where your heart aches over
"no"

and "not-yets" abound,
the Lord is near.

When you know the pain of
waiting firsthand,
or for one you love,
when there is
disappointment or you've
become disillusioned,
when there are questions or
doubt is the sea in which you
swim,
God is in your midst.

If uncertainty is your
certainty,
if questions eclipse answers,
if difficulty marks your path,
then these are the moments
where Peace keeps you safe,
protects your heart and
mind,
guards your fragile
existence.

CONTENTS

INTRODUCTION

I talk to dead people. Well, really, just *one* dead person. I talk to Eugene Peterson.

Maybe you know of him? Peterson was a small-town pastor who started translating the pages of Scripture for his congregation as part of his sermon-writing practice, only to emerge—years later—with a translation of the entire Bible that we now know as *The Message*. It's a poetic paraphrase, a dance of modern language and age-old ideas, a metaphoric goldmine of new ways to think about unchanging things, like God, and life, and life with God.

The Message has been my translation of choice for several years now, because it brings passages I've memorized in more familiar translations back to me, usually in new or unexpected ways. Peterson's fresh, colloquial language has helped me to read God's Word once again, as if I'm reading it for the first time.

Not only am I an enthusiast of *The Message*, I'm also a fan of the translator. So I talk to Eugene Peterson. I marvel at his word choices, give him a "woot woot" when his translation

opens up something new for me and delights my soul, and
I sound off to him when his modern prose steps on my
toes—which, I admit, is far too often. I have to tell you about
how I talk to Peterson, because the whole impetus for this
book came out of such a conversation. Peterson's word choice
in a particular passage in the book of James caused my soul to
pause:

> Consider it a sheer gift, friends, when tests and
> challenges come at you from all sides. You know
> that under pressure, your faith-life is forced into
> the open and shows its true colors. So don't try
> to get out of anything prematurely. Let it do its
> work so you become mature and well-developed,
> not deficient in any way. (James 1:2-4)

Conversation ensued.

*A "sheer gift," Eugene? Oh, come on. Tests and challenges
should be seen as nothing other than a gift? A sheer gift?
An unmitigated gift? This seems unrelatable, Eugene; a bit
of a stretch. Unreasonable, really.*

Of course, Peterson is silent during this exchange. And just so
you don't think I'm losing it, I will tell you now that Peterson
is *always* silent, so my conversations are a bit one-way.

Another exceptional spiritual writer, Barbara Brown Taylor,
has written, "Language is the deck of cards we have been given
to name our experience. There are hundreds of games we play
with it, but in the end there are only fifty-two cards."

So, now, come with me as I daydream for a moment: in my mind, I'm pulling up to a poker table with several favorite theologians and spiritual writers. This is quite a work of mental fiction, as I've only seen poker in the movies and in my dorm several decades ago, and I've never actually played a hand. But, if I were playing a sort of word-game-poker with Peterson and Taylor, here's how that might go:

To Peterson, I'd say, *I see your 'sheer gift' and I raise you the letter A.*

All those gathered round my imaginary poker table would be perplexed by how I want to play this hand, introducing a new letter in this way, so I'd lay my hand face up on the table and spread it, so they can see what I'm holding. I'm not bluffing, not today.

You see, I'm proposing a new framework to these friends, whom I've only known through books and from afar. The deck of fifty-two cards I'm using now to talk about God still sees tests and challenges as gifts—but gifts of another kind.

Here's my framework: I see these setbacks, the downsizing and disappointments of life, as *shear gifts*. I've swapped out that second E that Peterson chose for an A, shifting the adjective from *sheer* to *shear*, to bring another shade of meaning to his already challenging translation.

And what, you wonder, might a *shear gift* be? Since I've created this new pairing of vocabulary, allow me to further define my framework.

shear gifts (*n., plural*)

1. the gifts that come only after something
   we love has been yielded, a piece of what
   we counted on has been displaced, or when
   we feel somehow "less" than we felt last
   month, or last week, or yesterday.

2. the benefits, tangible and often
   intangible, that are bestowed in seasons
   where we feel certain we're losing
   ground. These are the gifts that
   arrive when we're quite sure we've been
   altogether forgotten.

Perhaps you read these definitions and feel unsure that such
gifts exist. Maybe you've yielded something you love and can't
identify any shear gifts just yet. Perhaps it feels too far from
where you stand, on ground that has shifted and seems to be
disappearing, to see that such a gift might be possible. You may
wonder, where is God when I'm being downsized? Where is
God when every offer we make on a home gets rejected? I want
to encourage you to keep an open mind; there was a time not
very long ago when I, too, could not name these shear gifts.

But these are precisely the gifts I want to talk about, because,
to be honest, I can't stop seeing and naming them these days.
I want to introduce the framework of shear gifts because I
believe we are feeling grief and loss like never before, and I
believe that God shows up in these seasons, too. Perhaps even
more so. But to name the gifts like these, we must cultivate

new eyes to recognize Him, and we must expand our hearts to respond to His work in us.

A Towering Fiddle Leaf Fig Tree

It took me a while to see the results of a "losing" season this way. The idea found me unexpectedly, amid the COVID pandemic, when I occupied myself by learning to grow things. (In fact, I think a whole new crop of plant people are emerging from that season!)

I'm a nurturer, and I needed to nurture *something* besides my husband and teens, who were growing weary of all my mothering tendencies in our close-knit quarters. I started to bring home plants to nurture, and somewhere along the way, I bought a fiddle leaf fig tree.

She was a massive beauty, coming into our home at over six feet in her most mature state, and she wasn't done growing. The rare visitors to our home commented without fail on her statuesque, healthy form and her explosive growth.

Soon she was not only towering past seven feet, but she was also bending beneath her own top-heavy weight. So many giant green leaves were being supported by a skinny pole of a base, and my motherly joy soon turned to worry: something's got to give. She can't stand up under this immense foliage much longer.

Sometimes life speaks to us that way, too, doesn't it?

Has your life ever screamed, "Help! I'm about to break! Release me from the weight of this situation, relationship, thing, hardship, job, obligation, expectation. . . ." Maybe life is screaming at you right now, and if so, I'm glad you're reading this book.

So I did what any good plant-parent would do: I googled how to prune a fiddle leaf fig. Then I found the appropriate lopping tool, typically reserved for outside work, and—with great decisiveness—I cut that girl back by a third.

Then, I mourned.

I was so sad, because she didn't look the same anymore! No more towering green goodness, saluting the ceiling like a yogie meant to bend with grace. Now, my fiddle leaf fig looked stark; abruptly interrupted, even. And I felt grief for her irreversible loss. I worried I had made a very big mistake by cutting her back with such abandon.

As it turns out, my fears were relatively short-lived. About a month later, she began to unfold a generous number of new green leaves. That's when I realized it: I'd given my fiddle leaf a *shear gift*. By rebalancing her form and removing the weight of all she'd produced, I was giving her the chance to reorient and bud again.

Isn't that chance to reorient and bud again also the very chance so many of us desperately need, as well?

> For who do you know that really knows you, knows your heart? And even if they did, is there anything they would discover in you that you could take credit for? Isn't everything you have and everything you are sheer gifts from God?

So what's the point of all this comparing and
competing? You already have all you need. You
already have more access to God than you can
handle. (1 Cor 4:7-8a)

Everything you have, everything you are. All of it, sheer
gifts from God. (Peterson, you're at it again.) If all of it is sheer
gift—if all of us is sheer gift—then, surely, there are also *shear
gifts* in seasons of loss and what feels like a diminished role or
presence, gifts that present themselves only after we're sure
the ground we stood on is somehow lost.

But how do we get our arms around the truths we desperately
need when we're also sitting with the disappointment of a life
that feels, in some ways, unrecognizable? How do we receive
drastic reshaping and name the new life that is soon to emerge?

Seeing a New Telos

There is a Greek word, *telos*, which means the principal aim
or the outcome. It doesn't quite have an equal in English, so I'll
stick with the Greek. Knowing our telos through setbacks and
difficulties is absolutely essential. And, more often than not, we
must challenge the telos we've unintentionally picked up.

One story we've likely adopted from the world around us is
that the telos of life is happiness. As Americans, at a young age
we rehearse the words from our Declaration of Independence,
"certain unalienable Rights, among these . . . the pursuit of
Happiness." This idea is deep in our subconscious.

Years ago, there was a remarkable movie that was actually
called *The Pursuit of Happyness*. While the movie was

exceptional and pulled on my heart in so many ways, I was left
at the credits with a renewed conviction that happiness cannot
be our chief pursuit, or our telos, as Christ-followers. That is
an American concept, not a biblical idea.

Of course, it isn't wrong to want to be happy! However, if
happiness is your telos—your end goal, the thing you're trying
to accomplish with the whole of your life—you will never be
able to count a season of suffering as joy. And biblically, we're
told to "count it all joy . . . when we meet trials of any kind."

In seasons where we've been cut back beyond recognition, it is
essential to remember that God redeems and restores, and that
is His ultimate telos. Of this, we can be certain.

Maybe you're wondering, why is this difficulty in my life?
Why are so many hard things happening to me? What is
Master-Gardener-God up to when I am losing limbs and
branches faster than a brittle old tree in a hurricane?

I'm not journeying your road, so I won't pretend to have
answers about your situation. But I will say this from some
hard-earned experience: I've seen people face the most difficult
things. I've walked alongside addicts and held the hand of
those transitioning from this life to the next. I've delivered
the hardest news of all, that a loved one is with Jesus now.
I've walked with those who have had a loved one die by
suicide, those who have lost people suddenly, and those who
have experienced a long and sorrowful goodbye. I've been
beside people through financially devastating things, job loss,
physical pain and suffering, and I've seen what happens in the
struggle and on the other side.

In that struggle, however, I've seen people come to a much deeper and resolute faith. I've seen friends and family of those suffering come to learn new levels of prayer and sharing burdens. I've watched God work deep in the heart of someone to bring surrender.

And I've seen God restore. Oh, the restoration I've seen—in my own life, and in the lives of those I've had the privilege of ministering alongside.

I won't attempt to answer the age-old question of why God allows suffering; so many have written deep words of truth on this topic. I will weigh in, however, on where God is in the midst of suffering: He is *with us*, never leaving us. He stands in the heartache with you right now, whatever that heartache might be. And while I've never been certain that God "takes" anyone from this earth, I am absolutely certain that He receives those who have named Him in faith.

I know times like these are hard! When we journey into the work, rather than just trying to get through the work, we begin to see and name these *shear gifts*. So, with the psalmist, I'm inviting you to "drop everything and listen, listen as He speaks" (Ps 95:7). Because just when you think you are losing it all, when you're looking at bare spaces, stark endings, and holes you can't fill back in, you may, in fact, be gaining the essential, *shear gifts* of the Kingdom.

God and Revelation

When we hear the word revelation, most of us think about the last book in the Bible. But there is a lot more revelation in our lives than just that book of Scripture! What revelation really means is the showing or *unveiling* of a truth or insight, the capacity to see something we hadn't seen before. God is constantly revealing His heart, character, and purposes to us.

Of course, we know that God reveals Himself in Scripture. As we delve into its pages and revel in the stories and precepts, we learn of the character of our unchanging, unfailing God. The psalms proclaim God's presence on our best and worst days, in favorable and unfavorable circumstances alike. We learn of God's heart for His people, and the ends to which He will go to see them come to know Him and be in communion with Him.

And, at the risk of inviting theological critique, we can also learn something about God as we spend time with other people—because God's image is on each person He has created. To be sure, it stretches us greatly to identify the image of God on someone who is unlike ourselves. We can be quick to see God in those with whom we agree, those who are shaped like us and share our perspectives. But when we encounter someone quite different, perhaps that is when we have the opportunity to learn even more about God. I've certainly experienced that myself.

We also have the opportunity to learn about God in nature. We see His boundless creativity, as well as His love for systems and symmetry. We can observe His power and also His whimsy. As we spend time in God's creation, we learn more about Him. (I know some theologians would want to quibble with me here, so let me quickly transition to something on which I believe we'd agree.)

The greatest revelation of God, however, is found in Jesus. Jesus shows us the heart of the Father, the character and will of God, like none other. Jesus put on flesh and dwelt among us; He "put on skin and moved into the neighborhood," as Peterson puts it. It follows, then, that the more we experience Jesus, the more we know of God.

I think about all these forms of revelation like the finding of pieces as we put together the puzzle of what we believe to be true about God. The more revelation we see and receive, the more we come to know God and His heart for us. Over a lifetime, we connect ideas and new revelation, which shape our theology - or what we think about who God is and how He is at work in the world around us.

What This Means for Suffering

Throughout the whole of Scripture, we see a repeated concept that a smaller thing is yielded for a greater thing. For instance, the Kingdom of God always has this multiplicative impact—a little yeast, when worked through dough, makes the whole batch rise. Or an incredibly tiny mustard seed, when it is buried in the ground, sprouts into an unwieldy tree—and it happens quickly. These Kingdom metaphors tell us something about how even a tiny Kingdom seed or a bit of Kingdom yeast can very quickly multiply.

We also know this to be true: in life, resurrection cannot happen without death. Nothing can be raised to new life without first experiencing death. We'd like it if we could skip over this step, wouldn't we? Churches tend to teach more on the triumphant resurrection than on the staggering loss that precedes it. However, we cannot get to the third day and the empty tomb without the suffering and the cross. Jesus submits to incredible suffering, and even death, in order to become for us the Resurrection and our Living Hope.

We can acknowledge this loss that Jesus faced, and even His death, as an incredible giving of Himself through suffering. We cannot identify with this side of Jesus, however, until we also have suffered—and even then, we can never *completely* identify with Him! As we face suffering and setbacks, we learn something very real about the character of Christ, who in the midst of the greatest suffering chose to stay the course, before rising in power to defeat the grave. This increased resonance with the humility and servanthood of Jesus is both a sign of spiritual growth and a *shear gift* that comes only after we suffer, only after we feel we are losing ground.

This view of suffering as another way that we experience revelation requires a shift in perspective: We tend to view suffering as something that may disprove the existence of a loving God. What if suffering, rather than disproving God's existence, serves to help us to understand more of Him? Might the revelation we receive in suffering about the heart of God and the depths of His love for us be like adding another piece to the building puzzle of our theology? It's worth spending some time with this concept, as you pray, by asking this question: *God, how are You revealing more of Yourself to me through this situation I am facing?*

New Paths

Sometimes, losing one path helps us to gain another way forward. The tricky part about this truth is that we see it most clearly in the rearview mirror, with perspective. It is difficult to look at a season of loss and think about how this setback may allow a new or different path to emerge. It becomes clear, though, after we've moved through the disappointment and have the perspective of looking back. This is why we often hear people testify to how one thing would never have happened if another hadn't happened first. It is always easier to name this dynamic *after* we've lived it, on the other side of the experience.

The new path that often emerges, however, is another *shear gift*. It can't come to be without the loss of another way forward. For instance, I pastored for a good season, which I thought might be my life's work. Only when I needed to step back from pastoring was I able to claim God's purpose in me to write. If it weren't for the loss of that place of ministry, I wouldn't be speaking into your life in this way right now. For me, this very book is a *shear gift*.

Now, it's my turn to hold space for you. Where in this current season of yielding might you also be receiving a shear gift? If you cannot name it in the present, could you pray for a heart that is open and for eyes to see and name it when it comes?

Here's the truth: God is always doing a new thing. We don't always perceive it, but that doesn't mean He isn't working. God is our Redeemer and Restorer. We don't have to be able to point to evidence today in our situation in order to claim the truth that this is who He is, so this is what is coming.

I'm learning to expect God to show up, bearing shear gifts I could never see coming. That is exactly who He is, and I've found that God never arrives empty-handed. In fact, He always seems to be carrying exactly what we each need at that very moment.

Let's choose trust.

The Waiting Room

What if the waiting room
you've been trying to escape
is actually a safe room?
If the holding pattern
you resist is really
the safest place for you to
rest?
If pushing out prematurely
would somehow put you
in harm's way?

What if,
instead of endlessly trying
to get out of this space,
you lay down to rest,
trusting the doors would
open
when the next thing was
ready,
and when you were ready,
too?

— · —

THE GROUND IN WHICH WE'RE PLANTED

1

—·—

THE STORIES WE TELL OURSELVES

"Faint-heart, what got into you?"
—Jesus to Peter, Matt 14:31

ele

Look Up
(based on Matt 14:22-33)

Faint-heart, what got into
you?
Did you look down to find the
ground
shifting again?
Sinking feet
cycle air to repeat
sure footing that isn't
coming.

Faith requires steps that
can't be

seen—measured—
mastered,
a
one-foot-in-front-of-the-
other
cadence into the deep,
disappearing feet and
sometimes
felling hearts and souls.

Don't you know, though?
He is next to you.
The One who speaks calm to
chaos,
the One who makes solid
ground appear
within waves of fury,
He is always there when the
going is rough.

Faint-heart, what got into
you?
Look up, friend;
Find your footing again.

There's a popular show called *How Stuff Works*—maybe
you've heard of it? This show has considerable longevity, as it
has been produced for over a decade! That's quite a collection

of hours documenting the insides of machines and mechanisms that deliver all the goods we use on a regular basis. If you've ever wondered how things get made, this show may be for you.

But what if there were an episode examining the spiritual life? I bet it would be the most viewed episode ever. After all, who doesn't long to know how spiritual life works, in more concrete terms? Wouldn't it be great to see exactly what happens first, and next, and how we get from point A to point B in our relationships with God?

While there are components and disciplines that assist in living abundantly in Christ, there is simply no straight line in spiritual growth. It looks different for each one of us, but rarely does it look something like this:

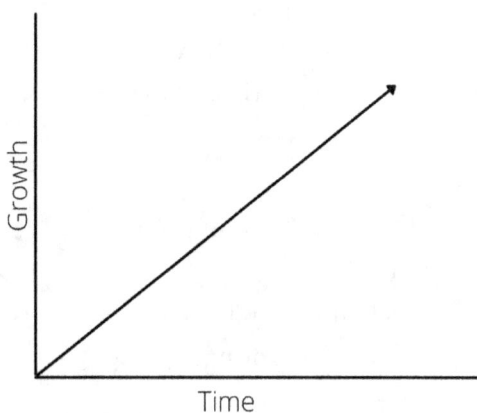

We'd love the straight-up-and-to-the-right line in our spiritual lives, wouldn't we?

I've been walking alongside people and their relationships with Jesus for several decades now, and the steady line up and to the

right is a myth. In fact, what we experience in our relationship
with Jesus usually looks something more like this:

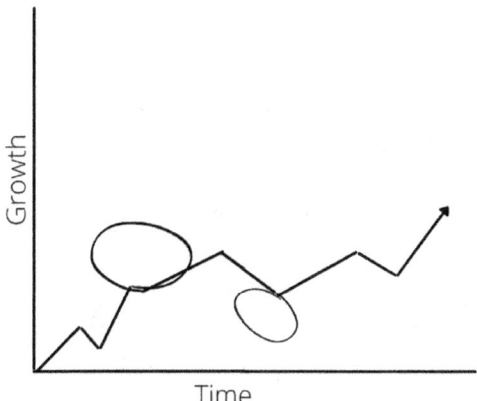

Your spiritual growth may have steeper climbs or drops, or even
times of plateau, but I believe it will rarely, if ever, look like the
straight-up-and-to-the-right line many so wistfully envision.

Maybe you're looking at that second image of the jagged,
loopy line and nodding your head, affirming your experience.
Perhaps, like most people I've met, you long for the
steady-up-and-to-the-right line of spiritual growth. Why
doesn't it happen that way for us, as people who are trying to
follow Jesus?

One element of this up-and-down spiritual life is the
give-and-take of living a life of faith in circumstances that
don't always seem to make sense. There is what we hope for in
this life, and then there is what we experience, which is usually
altogether different. When there is a disconnect between what
we hope for and what we see happening, our human hearts and

minds try to span that gap with some sort of idea about why that could be. You know the phrases I'm talking about:

- Everything happens for a reason.

- It's all good (when, in fact, it is clearly not!).

- Jesus just needed another angel in heaven.

- . . . (insert your own favorite, pithy phrase here).

Such theological gymnastics have us tumbling over and springing back. Rarely, however, do they enable us to stick a landing in the painful places of life and move through the hard places with real honesty. Such phrases are efforts to minimize pain, but God heals pain differently. Rather than minimizing our places of pain, He steps into it the hard stuff with us. His presence never leaves us; He walks beside us in the most difficult disappointment and heartache, rather than trying to get a running start and tumble over it to get to the other side. Consider Jesus' words:

> I've told you all this so that trusting me, you will be unshakable and assured, deeply at peace. In this godless world you will continue to experience difficulties. But take heart! I've conquered the world. (John 16:33)

Whoa. Did you hear that?

Jesus *guarantees* difficulty in this world. I know that is an uncomfortable fact for us to face, but it is true. Of course,

He also promises that He ultimately wins. So we can settle into this up-and-down, mountain-top-and-valley-low line and know that, even when the line dips significantly and it seems we are taking steps back spiritually, if we continue to lean in to our relationship with God, the line will ultimately be trending back up, because the promise is that in Christ, we are overcomers.

But how, then, does spiritual life *really* work?

Jesus speaks to our capacity to receive the Word and grow in it, producing a harvest, by describing soil. He describes how the Kingdom of God works using metaphors like yeast, mustard seeds, and a vineyard. Jesus picks these agricultural examples on purpose! These are the narratives Jesus uses, the kinds of stories He tells.

This is crucial for us to understand, because the modern world in which we live offers alternative stories for us to live, stories that we've probably adopted as lenses for seeing the world, without even realizing it. Adopting those stories as our lenses, even in subtle ways, affects the way we read Scripture and make sense of our faith lives.

Because of our often subliminal exposure to so many available stories that could, over time, shape our views of faith unhelpfully, we have some preconceived notions about how to bring about results in our lives in general, and we often apply these to our spiritual lives as well. These notions are largely based on our life experiences and the time in which we are living. The predominant stories we adopt shape our spiritual thinking in ways we can't always easily see or name.

These lenses can be problematic, because when we think we know how something works, we try to bring about results in the way we've understood (even subliminally) that they are achieved. We think X brings about Y, then Z, and we set out to prove that formula, which is rooted in a story we've come to believe or a way we've come to understand that life works. But what if we're applying a faulty formula or narrative, expecting an outcome that isn't going to come? Well, then we begin to feel disappointed or even disillusioned.

If we don't challenge some of these stories as they relate to our spiritual lives, we can't displace ideas about how we grow spiritually that are inaccurate and replace those with what Jesus says. I realize this all sounds really abstract! Let's look together at several dominant stories in our culture that, when adopted as our lenses on faith, challenge our ability to live out an abundant spiritual life.

The Industrial Manufacturing Story

Have you ever considered how the Industrial Revolution—the invention of machinery and the mechanization of processes that followed—might have impacted your spiritual life? We don't often think of industry and spirituality together, but it's amazing how much the former has impacted the latter.

As society shifted in the late 1700s and early 1800s from working the ground and making things by hand to employing machines that could do the work in a fraction of the time, and with endless and unyielding repetition, the world became a different place. Machines could do much of the work for people, and as those machines improved over time, we entered an era of unprecedented development, where production models shifted to assembly lines and the monitoring of machines that brought about increased output.

Of course, I'm simplifying the ways that innovation and technology have shifted the landscape of our lives, but Ford, Wegner, and Hirsch have written about how this industrial narrative has taken root in our hearts in ways that seem innocent, but absolutely shape our spiritual sensibilities.[1]

In this story, we manufacture. We are makers, and we bring about or produce results in a linear fashion and with efficiency. Like a machine, we put something in, and we get something out. Like an assembly line, we keep on doing the things, over and over, with speed and precision, and on the other end of that conveyor belt—*boom!* There is a product.

This works well in industry, but the spiritual life doesn't work like this.

Let that truth sink in for a moment. First, you may feel some disappointment: *you can't grit your teeth and make it happen.* You can't work harder, push through, and bring about some big spiritual growth or result in your life of faith. But the faulty part of this narrative is not simply that machines and spirits are different; it's that it isn't you, or me, who does the making!

If you wish you had more control over the outcomes in spiritual life, I feel you on this! Wouldn't we love for spiritual life to work the way so much of the world works, where we can keep control over outcomes and know that if we simply complete A, B, and C, then D will follow?

But as this truth that we can't manufacture spiritual fruit or outcomes takes up residence in our hearts and we learn to manage the fact that we can't manufacture our spiritual lives, it also offers us freedom. *We can't make it happen.* Do you hear how you're freed up even in the speaking of those words? We aren't the makers in this spiritual life; we are participants. We show up, and we are present. God meets us, and God does a work in us that we cannot do in ourselves. We yield ourselves to His work in us.

If we could do this spiritual work ourselves, Jesus would have offered some different metaphors. He was not bound by the understanding of people in the time in which he walked the earth; surely in His infinite knowledge, Jesus foreknew the coming capacity to manufacture. But Jesus doesn't say that the Kingdom of God is like a well-oiled machine. He also doesn't mention the Kingdom putting out widgets with precision, or an assembly-line approach to spiritual life. So let's set aside the idea of manufacturing our spiritual lives, because that is a faulty story for spiritual life, and that lens will limit our understanding of how growth happens.

The Performance Story

Hustle culture spins out a story that is quickly becoming an accepted paradigm, and unexamined way of life, in our time. Rather than saying rise and shine, hustlers say rise and grind. Put in the work, and when you think you're done—hustle harder. Many have come to believe that if it is to be, it's up to me.

The resulting performance story is a cousin to the industrial manufacturing story, but it moves us further in the direction of *performative workaholism*. The heart of this story is that we push harder and harder to become what we've decided we can be, and then, somehow it happens. At least, that's what this narrative promises. This lens says don't stop when you're tired; stop when you're done.

But the spiritual life doesn't work like this! We don't push hard to arrive at a spiritual destination; we're along for the ride with Jesus! In fact, Jesus says something that is quite the opposite of hustle culture mentality, as it relates to spiritual life:

> Are you tired? Worn out? Burned out on religion?
> Come to me. Get away with me and you'll recover
> your life. I'll show you how to take a real rest.
> Walk with me and work with me—watch how
> I do it. Learn the unforced rhythms of grace.
> I won't lay anything heavy or ill-fitting on you.
> Keep company with me and you'll learn to live
> freely and lightly. (Matt. 11:28-30)

Jesus offers us rest and renewal. He doesn't push us to keep moving when we're exhausted; Scripture tells us in Psalm 23 that God actually makes us lie down in green pastures, and that He restores our souls. So, let's put down the performance story, because it's a faulty lens through which to interpret the life of faith.

The Digital Story

We're all living in a time where digital life is on the rise, and there is an app for just about everything. In digital life, we have a great deal of control as consumers, adding and deleting that which serves us in the moment. Online, we curate an image to present to the world. In essence, we pick what we show to others. We control the narrative about ourselves in ways that are, again, subtle and often overlooked.

Spiritual life is also not like this! God isn't One who likes or drops hearts on our daily posts for the ways we present ourselves to Him. God isn't looking at your Facebook or Insta scroll. He is seeing all of you—the good, the not-so-good and everything in between. Let that truth sink into your heart and mind, because it's become easy to think of God as a consumer of our feed, and to manage what we share with Him, as though He sees only that—or would only love us for our good fruit.

The opposite is true, spiritually. In fact, even before you were born and named, you were known completely by God. Every aspect of your existence is encompassed by the Lord! Even for those who haven't yet known and named God, make no mistake about it: He knows and names every one of them. And His knowledge of us is intimate and complete.

The sooner we realize that there is no image-maintenance with God, the sooner we can relax in His presence and allow the truth to take hold: He knows everything about you, and He loves you today, right where you are, wherever you are. With Jesus, we need not amplify the best parts of ourselves and hide the worst parts. Rather, we bring our whole selves into His presence for healing, because nothing can separate any of us from His love! Not anything you've done, or failed to do. Not any choice you've made, not anything you've missed or failed to be. He loves you completely, right now, right where you are.

In much the same way, Jesus can heal anything we bring into His presence. He heals our hearts, our minds, our souls, and Jesus redeems every aspect of our lives that we submit to Him. The opposite, of course, is also true; what you don't bring to Jesus does *not* come into His healing light and love. His part is the healing, and our part is the bringing. Friends, Jesus respects you, and He waits for you to bring yourself completely to Him. He gives us the free will to choose what we surrender, and when we do it, as well. Whenever you bring it to Him, healing begins. Until you bring it fully to Jesus, healing waits.

Another aspect of the digital story is that we sometimes want to coopt *someone else's* story. Ever see something great in someone else's feed, and then try to create it in yours?

We are all collectors of stories; it's part of being human. There are only two stories we can live in our spiritual lives, however—our own story with God and the story that Jesus invites us into (which is so much bigger and better than anything we could ever dream). Spiritually trying to live another's story, curating experiences that look like some other online influencer, is an empty promise that brings about nothing but momentary imitation. Our faith must be our own—not our pastor's, parent's, sibling's, or best friend's faith-on-loan.

Your story with Jesus is the very best story you will ever live. Let's put down the digital lens and stop trying to manage our image with God. We were meant for more than that! There is a better way.

Agriculture Is Still the Right Metaphor

I can hear you asking, if all of these other stories that we know and easily name are not right for spiritual life, what is the *right* lens through which to see the life lived by faith?

The best metaphor is (of course!) the one that Jesus used repeatedly: an agricultural one. But it's important to know something about this agricultural way of understanding faith—namely, we must understand our role in the metaphor. We're not the farmer. Not the gardener. Not the caretaker. Not the one managing the field.

You and I are the *soil* in which the Great Gardener, who is God, plants seed. We are the field that is plowed up and worked by the Faithful Farmer. We are also the vines, Jesus tells us, connected to the One True Vine that is Jesus. We are like trees that bear fruit. We are what the seed produces. But we are never the producer—that is God's role in the story.

The beautiful part about this agricultural storyline is that it also holds space for all the things we cannot control. Just like when seeds are planted in the ground, we can't control so much of what happens around us, but the Good News here is that it isn't even our job. Our job is to receive what Jesus has done for us and respond in faith. Our job is to receive what God has next for us and respond to the Spirit's work in our lives. To do that, we must stay spiritually connected.

One More Thing

In this book, we will talk a lot about time. If you've purchased this book, you're probably living in a time where you feel you are losing ground, and I realize that means different things to different readers. Maybe for you that is a loss of spiritual ground, or maybe you've lost something you hold dear, like a person or a relationship, or perhaps a job. Maybe you're walking through a medical diagnosis that represents lost ground. Maybe your finances are in shambles. Perhaps you're reading this book because it seems like a lot has changed, and it isn't a change for the better.

No matter what reasons you have for reading this book right now, I invite you to evaluate your experience with two trusty comrades: grace and truth. These are other, biblical ways of seeing; I think of grace and truth as bookends on our lives that help us to know more about a life of faith and grow spiritually.

Truth helps us see where change is needed and where we must realign our lives in light of God's love. *Grace* includes the gifts of God that bring us to this time and enable us to be open to and receive the change that is needed.

When we evaluate our experience with grace and truth, we are living in what Dr. Henry Cloud calls "good time."[2] In good time, change is possible. When we withhold our experiences and do not bring them into God's light of grace and truth, our lives continue unchanged, despite the passage of time. Dr. Cloud points to this time as an unproductive time, spiritually. It's like living the same year over and over. No one wants to do that; we want to grow. But in order to grow, we must bring our whole selves to spiritual life and allow grace and truth to inform our steps.

Let's let these pages represent, then, our initiative toward living in good time, where change is possible in light of God's

truth and grace working in us. I invite you to bring your whole
self here—and I will try to do that, too.

On Grace

It's easy to mistake grace for
a window
casting light through a
slight frame,
far more outside than can
get in
but by positioning yourself
just right
you might find a sliver of
grace
for minutes, or a moment—
like a warm sunny spot
before the Source moves.

But that's not a grace-full
life at all.

Here is a joyful discovery:
Grace is a wide-open door
inviting us all to cross the
transom
and enter spaciousness,

illuminating the deep
comforts
of God's boundless love
and the peace of finding
Home.

---

1. Lance Ford, Rob Wegner, and Alan Hirsch, The Starfish and the Spirit (Grand Rapids, MI: Zondervan, 2021), 174.

2. Henry Cloud, Changes that Heal (Grand Rapids, MI: Zondervan, 2018), 45.

2

DYNAMIC SOIL

Pandemic Poetry: the Grocery Store

Confession: I used to like
grocery shopping
I'd get lost in aisle three
pouring over teas
and find odd satisfaction in
procuring all the things.
And so I can name it now:
Nothing is the same.
Not even the grocery store.
As I carefully pull the mask
over my ears
I prepare to begin.
There is a list now, because
nothing can be forgotten
or I have to risk it all again to
return,
and the risk feels great.

Spontaneity has become an
enemy.
Spritz, spritz: I wipe down
my cart.
Five weeks into this and I'm
still surprised
by so many bare shelves,
empty liners where poultry
and ground beef go,
still no toilet paper,
weird things now scarce
like baker's yeast and
sometimes bananas.
What will be missing
tomorrow?
Only half the haul is found,
so onto
a second store, the whole
routine again.
Is it just me, or are prices
rising?
Scarcity does that, you
know;
demands a higher price,
drives up fear.
Last, the checkout.
Peering through plexiglass,
six feet away,
the most disturbing thing of
all is now easy to name.
Mouths hidden under masks,

weary eyes remind me that
we are all so tired.
It isn't the empty shelves or
the care required
to complete a once simple
task that undoes me.
The scarcity that I most feel
is now front and center.
Confession: What I miss
most are smiles.

Depending on when you are reading this chapter, maybe we're emerging from a global pandemic. But then again, as we've learned to adapt our expectations, maybe not. We've become all too familiar with the language of variants. New strains. And the fact that, with time, despite science and vaccines, protection may wane.

We are left in this never-ending samba dance where we shift from side to side: first cases seem to be trending down which means things are better, and then things are getting worse, and we should mask up and keep six feet apart. Now, remove the masks and we can hug our friends and family again. Wait, someone was sick and didn't know it, now we are all quarantining because of close contact. Sound familiar?

The resulting choreography is confusing to the mind, body, and soul.

It felt untrue to write a book about losing ground amid a pandemic and not address the role of the pandemic in that real and felt loss. That would be like not acknowledging the elephant in the room, and we've all seen this elephant—and not just her trunk or her wiry tail, either. Over time, we've seen the whole, massive gray beast occupying our space.

Throughout this pandemic, many of us have experienced loss that is concrete, and though it is incredibly difficult to live through, loss like this is quite easy to name:

- loss of a loved one to COVID or a complication of COVID;

- long COVID and the resulting medical uncertainty it brings;

- loss of income or career opportunity due to quick shifts in market demands;

- mental health concerns following long periods of required quarantine or isolation;

- increasing responsibility at home with decreasing support outside of the home; and

- wearing multiple hats as caregivers and career-builders, and the loss of self in this strained time.

The list goes on and on.

Collectively, we've seen what a pandemic can do to the physical, mental, and emotional self, and it is hard, and scary. We've seen losses like the ones just named, and the domino-like effect in our personal worlds from the falling of one spotted-ivory tile.

But what exactly does a pandemic do to the deepest parts of our souls? For certain, the ground beneath us has shifted. I believe that shifting ground has also impacted our sense of grounding, the very soil of our souls. The pandemic has deeply affected our spiritual selves, and the sooner we acknowledge that, the sooner we can move back toward a healthier spiritual life.

Grounded in Time

Grounding is important for humankind. As humans, we do best when we can count on certain things that frame the way we see the world and the lives we live. Collectively, and individually, we're grounded by a number of things, including how we understand and relate to time and space. Although we may have not named the ways we relate to the calendar, ongoing and regular appointments, rhythms, and routine in our lives as a stabilizing force, once these things were suddenly taken away, it became clear how we'd counted on them. As the old adage says, you don't know what you've got until it's gone.

Remember those first weeks of the pandemic? As we slowly realized what was happening in the world, and how quickly COVID would make its way to our continent and lives, things rapidly shut down. The very way that we move through our days, including our routines and rhythms, were suddenly and simultaneously disrupted. Calendars became unrecognizable; our social life shrunk to the size of virtual interactions while surrounded by those with whom we share a living space. Unable to come and go freely and without fear of this spreading disease, our world changed overnight—and for far longer than any of us initially anticipated.

We humans are always thinking in terms of time. We reflect on things as before and after, then and now, years ago and today, or perhaps—always and suddenly. The pandemic has impacted that last set of words; the things we always counted on were suddenly taken away.

When it comes to time, we understand it as expressed in days, weeks, and months. We also comprehend time through seasons, although, depending on our geography, those seasons may vary. In the shortest terms, we process time through minutes and seconds. Qualitatively, we think in terms of moments—especially moments that matter deeply, which we tend to mark with others in community.

The pandemic brought about a sense of blurred time.[1] Less activity in our days led to an increased focus on free time to fill, and, as a result, many of us felt that time slowed down.

Time perception is shaped not only by what is happening *around* us, but also what is happening *within* us: our internal clock ticks to an established pace and rhythm. That is, until it doesn't.

When events are canceled and calendars empty, we feel the resulting loss of what used to fill our days, as well as grief about not having what we've looked forward to doing. Do not underestimate this challenge to our very nature as humans; blurred time results in disorientation. That's only part one, though, of the shifting ground of a pandemic.

Grounded in Spaces

We've also lost our connection with many spaces in our lives, including important spaces that hold emotional weight and connect to our daily existence in deeper ways than we may realize. For most of us, the pandemic has resulted in far more time at home, which means that a space with a primary purpose of living quarters quite suddenly took on additional freight, as the container for secondary and tertiary purposes, like work, school, and worship.

Asking one space to do so many things is taxing, not only on the space itself but also on the occupants of this space. If time has been blurred for many of us, spaces become blurred as well. Do I live here? Sleep here? Work here? Worship here? Teach my kid here? Do all of my shopping here? Never leave these walls? Where does my workday end and my family life begin? How do I shift to engage in worship without going to the building where I'm accustomed to experiencing this? How do I keep kids on task, or myself on task, with so many easy distractions at my fingertips?

I hope that, as you are reading this, you are realizing once more just how much you've lived through in this incredibly challenging and life-changing time of a global pandemic.

The places that are important in our lives are more than just physical buildings; certain spaces hold an emotional attachment for us and bring about a set of feelings associated with the place. Our strong feelings and attachment to certain places play significant roles in how we experience our sense of identity.[2] So the sudden loss of key places and spaces in our lives impacts our sense of rootedness, and it challenges our identity as it has been understood in relation to these spaces.

The Soil of a Heart

When Jesus taught about the condition of our hearts, he used a metaphor of soil to help us understand how we receive and respond to Him. You can find this parable three places in the gospels, but we'll look at it in Mark, the fourth chapter:

> "Listen. What do you make of this? A farmer planted seed. As he scattered the seed, some of it fell on the road and birds ate it. Some fell in the gravel; it sprouted quickly but didn't put down roots, so when the sun came up it withered just as quickly. Some fell in the weeds; as it came up, it was strangled among the weeds and nothing came of it. Some fell on good earth and came up with a flourish, producing a harvest exceeding his wildest dreams.
> Are you listening to this? Really listening?"
> (Mark 4:3-9)

This is an essential teaching when it comes to spiritual life and growing in faith, so we're going to pitch a tent and camp out here for a couple of chapters. We're going to examine this text and our own, post-pandemic, spiritual condition, as we really consider various kinds of soil. After all, soil is not static, so the condition of the soil in our hearts is always up for change. (If you're feeling disconnected spiritually right now, this is good news: the soil of your heart can be changed for the better!)

Maybe this is a new idea for you? It can be tempting, in faith-life, to think of a decision to follow Christ as a permanent establishment of the good soil. If you've made a decision for Christ, you've received the seed that was sown, right? Yes, you've received the initial seed. However, discipleship is about a constant reorientation to receive and respond in spiritual life, and that requires the soil of our hearts to stay receptive and healthy.

Ground soil is dynamic. Over time, scientists tell us that soil responds to five things: climate, organisms, the landscape, parent material, and time.[3]

I don't think this was an accidental metaphor that Jesus picked for us; I think Jesus chose soil to represent what's happening in our hearts because his listeners understood it intimately, and they had their hands in it many, if not most, days. They'd certainly worked with soil that was hardening, or getting rocky, or weed-ridden. This was both a vivid metaphor and a real-life experience for the listener. They knew the perils of planting in subpar soil. That would absolutely impact the ability of the seed to flourish and produce an abundant crop.

Jesus was sharing ideas about how the heart receives through a metaphor that was easily understood by His audience. But it is also a metaphor that holds true through every part of the application. Let's dig into a couple of the factors that impact soil and open ourselves up to consider how the soil of our hearts may have changed with the many factors that impacted us in recent years.

Climate

How has the "prevailing set of conditions" changed for us recently?[4] (I literally saw you just roll your eyes. Yes, we are going there. We must! Here goes.)

We've already covered how our very sense of grounding has changed as we've related so differently to both time and space through the course of the pandemic. But the challenge to our conditions doesn't stop there, does it?

One morning, we wake up and start naming what's been lost. We could name it for hours, for days. So much has changed. We realize that everything seems familiar, but nothing is the same. Change isn't the hard part; it's the sense of loss that makes change feel nearly unbearable, untenable to us.

Perhaps the change in climate is best described by an acronym that was first used by economists in 1985, but seems to have more relevance today than ever before.[5] The term, VUCA, was then used in the 1990s by the US Army War College following the collapse of the USSR. If you're wondering how this sort of history might speak to the time in which we're living now, consider this acronym.

VUCA stands for Volatile, Uncertain, Complex, and Ambiguous. We'll take those one by one to consider what each word really means:

The world in which we are living is volatile. Volatile things are difficult to capture and hold; they are rapidly changing. The world definitely feels difficult to capture and hold right now.

It's also uncertain, meaning our daily life is full of surprises. Not all of these surprises feel good, do they? But we aren't quite sure what is coming next, and that feeling brings about a level of anxiety in most people.

The letter C represents complex. Never before have we had to manage so many different priorities or sync so many moving parts. New elements emerge on the regular, and we must fold them into our existing lives. In short, everything has gotten a bit harder in the last several years, requiring more thought and intention for even our simpler tasks.

Finally, ambiguity surrounds us. There is more than one way forward, and it isn't always clear which way is right. We may choose one path after much deliberation, only to have that path disappear and a new path emerge.

In the midst of a VUCA world, one of two things happens, spiritually speaking: our souls shrink or our souls expand. There is no neutrality in this territory; no one is holding ground in a state of sameness, spiritually, when the world is changing so quickly. Our faith lives are dynamic, just like the soil. They are changing in response to these conditions, reacting to the climate we are emerging in. Either we are changing for the good or this climate has had a negative impact on us, eliciting a shrinking of the soul. More and more as I talk to people, I'm hearing them reflect on how they find themselves in that latter category.

I've always been a fan of the slow cooker. Put something in mid-morning; serve a delicious meal at dinnertime. This literally got me through feeding a family in the early years of parenting! A number of years ago, though, a new device showed up called the Instapot.

I'm sure you are familiar, as I think most kitchens have some version of this all-in-one, quick working pressure cooker. Unlike the slow cooker, when I put a cut of meat into the Instapot, it cooks really, really fast. This is because of the kind of pressure that the Instapot employs. It's a high-heat, high-pressure environment, and results are instantaneous in that sort of space.

Many of us want to blame the pandemic for our condition—the place we find ourselves in life, and especially in spiritual life. But here's the truth: before COVID came along, we were slow cooking in life. COVID, however, placed us inside an Instapot, with much more heat and pressure than we're accustomed to. Whatever direction we were already moving, the pandemic accelerated it. The pandemic has gotten us more quickly to the place we were already trending. The pandemic has been an Instapot for our spiritual lives, and now we are seeing the results. The good news is that God's mercy is new every morning. So, we can always, always, always begin again.

Landscape

Some time ago, I used to run regularly in a beautiful park. This particular park has great trails, and it was close to our home, so I would head out for a jog on the trails several times a week. I knew the trails quite well, or so I thought. Then we moved to a new home.

We didn't move far, but my running routes changed accordingly. One day, after a number of months had passed, I decided it could be fun to go for a run again on those old trails. I missed the park! I was eager to return.

Initially, the run was exhilarating, and the trails felt like home. There were all the familiar elements, winding along by the river. I nodded to the tree that bowed to nearly touch the gravel path, circled the large stump around the bend, and I admired the tall grass to my right.

However, not only had time passed, but there had also been a big storm since my previous visit. The landscape had changed! Trees that once served as markers had been downed or were missing altogether. The changes were subtle, but they impacted my ability to perceive what I'd known before. So, as I navigated the twists and turns of the trails, I suddenly felt quite disoriented: All at once, everything was similar, and yet nothing was the same.

Those are the words I'd use to describe spiritual life, as well as life amid a global pandemic. Everything seems similar, but nothing is quite the same. Even in the most familiar parts of our lives, new demands or concerns layered over old experiences make life feel familiar but distant. Our spiritual lives can learn something from our pandemic experiences.

The Almighty Sower Never Stops

There is something we must consider, though, about this soil metaphor before we start to look closely at those soil types, and that is the Sower. Imagine for a moment that you hired someone to seed your yard, and then you came home to find the seed all over every surface? Imagine that there was seed on the gravel, and on the rocks, seed on the road and the sidewalk, and everywhere in between. I imagine you would have some choice words for the sower.

But that's exactly what happens here. The Sower in this parable is God, who is sowing the Word. (Jesus tells us that when he explains this parable to His disciples.) But God is a bit of an extravagant Sower, is He not?

He isn't judging who is ready to receive the seed. He's not sowing only where the soil is deemed good and the hearts are sure to be ready. Rather, God is sowing the seed of His word in all the places. (All the places!!) And all the time. (All the time!!)

This is worth a pause. This is worth serious consideration. In our humanness, we tend to think about sowing into plots that seem productive; every other sort of sowing would seem a waste. However, God's sowing initiative in this parable shows us that all soil is fair game.

This extravagant sowing is an example of a profound biblical truth: God is always the initiator in our spiritual lives. We may think we've turned toward Him, and that was our doing. But any time we turn toward God, it is always in response to His presence, which is already there. We don't summon God when we are ready to change, spiritually—it is exactly the opposite. God is always wooing us; God never stops sowing. He is summoning you right now, calling you close, even as you read these words. He initiates, and we respond. He plants, and we grow. He tends the soil, and we bring our whole selves to the process. He tills the ground, and we receive that turning over of the ground. He prunes, and we are better for it. God alone initiates. And God is always working, even when we can't see how He is working or what He is doing.

Anywhere in life that you've left footprints, God has left fingerprints. His love for us knows no bounds. So, let's talk about soil. Because it might be time to examine what's happening in our hearts, post-pandemic, and to allow the Holy Spirit to reveal some places where there is work to be done, so your soil is ready to receive again. The best part of this parable that Jesus tells is that he actually immediately spells out the meaning of it for his disciples. We are modern-day disciples, and this soil analogy has a lot to say to us.

> "Are you listening to this? Really listening?"
> (Mark 4:9)

—ele—

Gardener God

Gardener God,
The things I've counted on
are suddenly sideways
and I think—
Are they ever going to turn
up again?

All the friends
I no longer see

evidence of something
I used to be
and the ground seems to
have shifted beneath me.

I'm less worried about
catching what's in the air
And more concerned with
emerging with my soul
intact
When the world tips
turns and dips
we realize at different times
that what we counted on
was temporal.

But deep in me is the need
for something far more
eternal:
To be rooted completely in
the soil of
One who is immovable
when everything else is
moving.

Ground me again, Gardener
God.
Transplant me, if You deem
it needed.
I trust Your hands to hold
together the frail roots

of my being.
I trust Your hands to hold
together the pieces of this
life.

---

1. Simon Grondin, Esteban Mendoza-Duran, and
   Pier-Alexandre Rioux, "Pandemic, Quarantine, and
   Psychological Time," Frontiers in Psychology October 20,
   2020, /.
2. Maria Vittoria Giuliani, "Theory of Attachment and
   Place Attachment," in Psychological Theories for
   Environmental Issues, edited by M. Bonnes, T. Lee, and
   M. Bonaiuto (Aldershot: Ashgate, 2003), 137–70..
3. https://www.soils.org/about-soils/basics/.
4. https://www.merriam-webster.com/dictionary/climate/.
5. https://www.vuca-world.org/where-does-the-term-vuca-
   come-from/.

3

ROCKY SOIL, SHALLOW ROOTS

**True Discipleship
(based on Isaiah 46)**

Humans favor small gods
the kind we create and name
we can talk to them and they
won't talk back:
no loving correction
no guiding direction.
Most people want to make
their own way.

So much harder it is to follow
the Incomparable
to serve the Creator whose
ways we can't fathom
to recognize the One who
names us with wild accuracy
before we even know
ourselves.

True discipleship is giving
oneself fully
to the True God
and falling into His plan,
rather than asking Him to
fall into yours.

And some are like the seed that lands in the gravel.
When they first hear the Word, they respond with
great enthusiasm. But there is such shallow soil
of character that when the emotions wear off and
some difficulty arrives, there is nothing to show
for it. (Mark 4:16-17)

Gravel. Rocks. Stones. Pebbles. These are things you don't
want to see when you get ready to plant in a garden or
a field. Rocks and stones make great borders, because they
delineate where things grow from where things don't. Gravel
is an excellent path-maker, because when you put it down, it
discourages the continuance of anything green that may have
been beneath. That's how rocky ground works; it discourages
growth.

This troublesome soil seems to be as much about the presence
of the rocks as it is the absence of the roots, though, in the
way that Jesus explains this kind of heart condition. The gravel

works against the depth of the roots. So, we will talk about the rocks, and we must also consider these shallow roots.

An interpretation of gravel for this turbulent time

Jesus clearly shows that rocky soil is initially responsive. The problem is that the roots just don't endure. Many commentators would point toward trials as the reason the seed doesn't survive. Hard times come, or, as Jesus says, "difficulty arrives," and the seed withers.

I've reflected on all of this at length, and I'd like to offer you some fresh thoughts about rocks and roots in our spiritual lives. Many people have written about the rocks as trials. I'm thinking instead, however, about spiritual desperation in the hardest seasons, poor substitutes for Jesus, and what happens in our hearts when we allow stones to impede deep roots.

There's no doubt that we are living in a time of hardship. Many, many things are difficult right now. They press on us in ways we've possibly never experienced before. There is a cumulative weight to the pressure that is most difficult to endure. Any time a system is under pressure, it seeks relief.

Cue the rocks.

Looking for a Way Out

More than perhaps any other time that I've lived, I see people looking for the way through or—at a minimum—a way out. Some of the patterns are predictable; we humans tend to be oriented toward seeking out places of less pain and pressure when given the opportunity. No one signs up for ongoing difficulty in life. Increased pressure and circumstantial weight

makes us seek out a way out. Anything that might offer relief is
on the table for most people. What's the next, new thing? We
can insert it here and know that people are trying that thing.
Disciples are not immune from the desperation for relief. Let's
remember that we are exactly human-sized.[1]

This is where I think so many of the rocks we're dealing
with have slipped in. Yes, there is a trial. But there is also
the overwhelming desire to be *out* of this difficult time: *What
works? Got anything to offer? I'll try it. If you say it might
help, I'll do it.*

The Desire to Escape

One of the ways we humans numb our pain is by trying to
escape, even for a moment, to a better, lighter, happier place.
There are all sorts of escape options in the world in which we
live.

Sometimes we escape through a favorite show, or movie, or
some form of media. When it offers a sense of relief, we engage
again. Next thing we know, we are binge watching; our brains
have cued into this sense of relief, and we are hooked. We carry
around our phones and devices as though what is playing on
them might be a portal out of this hard place.

Another form of escape comes through substances. Ever
wonder why marijuana has suddenly become so socially
acceptable, seemingly overnight? I think the pandemic had
something to do with it: don't underestimate the power of a
mind-altering drug in a time when people are desperate to
alter their minds, even for a moment. Glass of wine to relax?
Turned into several, or more? It's an escape mechanism. If

you find yourself here, you're not alone. In a recent study, 17 percent of people report heavy drinking as a regular practice during the pandemic.[2] Think about it: that is almost 1 in 5.

Gaming offers another place for our minds to land, and a seductive sort of place, where we can win at something again. Pornography, too, is another highly addictive escape from reality; it was a common vice before the pandemic, but now this addiction is even more sharply on the rise. Shopping can be an escape, where retail therapy extends a sense of well-being for a moment.

All these trends are well documented. Consider this excerpt from *Frontiers in Psychiatry* to further illustrate the global trend toward escapism during the pandemic:

> BBC and Netflix recorded 16 million new subscribers in the first 3 months of 2020, almost 100% higher than the new subscribers during the last few months of 2019. In April, Microsoft's game servers had 10 million users, showing how the internet gaming industry has thrived in the pandemic. A preliminary study in China comparing data between October 2019 and March 2020 reported a sharp increase (23%) in the prevalence of severe internet addiction with a 20-fold rise in the dependence degree of those already addicted to the internet. Another study conducted in China limited to adolescents depicted a rise in internet use, especially in subjects considered as "Addictive Internet

Users" based on the questionnaire's cutoff. A
cross-sectional study in Taiwan claimed that the
prevalence of internet addiction in adolescents
was much higher than other previously recorded
samples worldwide.[3]

The truth is that most anything can be an escape, when it is
used as one. Even good things can be overused as an escape
from life.

All the escape plans we've made, whether for the pandemic or
just life in general, have become like rocks in the soil of our
lives. These escape rocks have become like permanent fixtures,
lulling us into underfunctioning and impeding our growth.
We've allowed them a place in the soil of our hearts, and we
return to these rocks of escapism again and again. But they
don't have to stay that way. We just need to see them, name
them, and begin to displace them.

The Perceived Need to Control

Maybe escape hasn't been your mindset. There is another kind
of rock I see popping up everywhere these days, and that is any
rock that might help people feel like they are in control again.
Uncertainty fuels the desire to regain control, and we've all
had more than our fair share of uncertainty in the past several
years.

What would those rocks of control look like? Think back
to when the pandemic began: Were you someone who
immediately seized a plan, perhaps with some intense goals?
Did you decide to reorganize your entire home while you were
quarantining? Learn a new language? Complete a detox or

cleanse? Master Tai Chi? (Okay, I'm smiling over here, and I hope you are, too.)

Sometimes the rocks of control show themselves in an overwhelming suspicion about anything and everything in life. Sometimes it is basic overfunctioning; we can do twelve things for the people around us who are not doing much, and if we keep spinning all the plates, it looks like we're wildly productive and in control.

Control can be seen in image maintenance, and even in overplanning. My pantry *might* offer up evidence of some of my desire to control; overpurchasing as a way of hedging my bets against possible future scarcity on the grocery store shelves seems to be a control rock in my life.

Maybe you relate more to the need to control than the need to escape. I find that most people locate themselves somewhere on this continuum, and at least one of these behaviors is relatable. If you see evidence of both control and escape in your life recently, take heart; here come the traveling companions you need. You're in the right place for some grace and some truth. Remember those friends? Truth is coming first.

Hope Always Has an Object

Any time we are waiting on something or hoping for something, there is always a "something." In other words, we can't hope without having something to hope for. We place our hope in all sorts of things: sometimes our hopes are in things we can't easily name. For instance, we've just named two possible objects of our hope: escape and control.

When we place our hope in escape, we're hoping for something that will take away pain, even for a moment. We're hoping for release. It would be so great if that release were permanent! But we know deep down, when we choose to hope in escape, that it's temporary. What we haven't yet named is that escape is a lying hope.

That's right: it lies.

Escape promises a way out that it cannot give. It overpromises, and underdelivers. In the moments after trying to escape, you might feel guilt, sadness, a profound emptiness, shame, embarrassment, or even a hangover. But I can guarantee you this: you won't feel better.

In equal parts, control is a lying hope. When we place our hope in control, we're hoping for something that will let us call the shots, even in small ways.

Control promises something that is impossible; it invites you to hope in a perfectly ordered world that exists just the way you planned it. That plan exists only in one place—your perfect plan exists only between your ears.

You may force some things into being when you work hard to control what is uncontrollable. But there always comes a time—always—where you cannot make something happen.

That's because we really don't control much at all, do we? If you've ever read Stephen Covey's seminal work, there's a small circle of what we can control in life (our circle of influence) and a much larger circle of what we have little to no control over (circle of concern).[4] So hoping in our ability to control when so much of life falls beyond what we can even influence is choosing to put our faith in a lying hope.

When we allow lying hopes to take up residence in the soil of our heart, they begin to edge out growth. For some of us, we've tried one or both of these things—and we may have also tried faith during this season. But the seeds of faith germinate and grow in good soil.

When these other, lying hopes, are present, they smother out the seed of faith—which is our only Living Hope.

Displacing Rocks and Lying Hopes

How do we displace rocks that have become lodged in soil? If you've ever done this work, you know it requires some digging and some manual displacing. This is work that happens on your knees, close to the soil. It's work that requires perseverance, not to mention a partner in the Holy Spirit, someone who helps you to see these lying hopes and move them out of the soil bed of your heart.

Sometimes I begin with a journal and a few, simple questions: What have I been placing my hope in during this difficult season? What does that look like on a daily basis? (And I get specific!) What do I need to change in order to displace these rocks?

As you sit with those questions, try asking the Holy Spirit to shine a light on your heart and raise up the places of concern, so you can see them clearly. Then, as things come to mind, capture them on paper. Naming the lying hopes in your life is essential in the work of displacing them.

Once you've got a list of places you've been prone to place your trust that are not the Living Hope of Jesus, it's time to confess them specifically to God—and repent. Now, those are two rather churchy words, so I'll take a moment to spell this out: when you confess the sin, you name it back to God and tell Him how you're struggling with it. You tell Him that this is a lying hope, and you want to trust only in His Living Hope. You ask for His help to make a change!

Repenting means not only acknowledging the sin, but actually turning from it. When we repent, we make a 180-degree turn from the thing that has been a problem. What might that look like in your life, practically? Here are some ideas:

- Delete the app that is tripping you up.

- Put a safeguard on your screen to keep you from going to a site that has caused problems.

- Remove substances used for escape from your home if you're prone to overusing them.

- Make an appointment to get the help of a professional counselor, or a doctor, depending on your need.

- Get accountability outside of yourself—join an AA program, or talk to a friend and let them know where you've been struggling. Invite accountability and help.

- Freeze your credit card in a block of ice if you're prone to overusing it.

- Admit the places you've tried to assert control and ask for accountability around those behaviors and choices.

This is what true repentance looks like; it isn't just a heartfelt desire to stop a destructive pattern. True repentance is turning from the pattern, and that requires an element of action in our lives that may seem bold in the moment, but you'll be so much better for it.

How do we make these changes? Well, this is where grace comes in. Grace is a big part of what animates change in us; God helps us in ways we cannot always know, but His grace motivates and sustains us in places where we are turning from old patterns. 2 Cor. 12:9 puts it this way, "My grace is enough; it's all you need. My strength comes into its own in your weakness."

Come, Lord Jesus

I am learning a new prayer,
three little words
with immense power,
pregnant with possibility:
Come, Lord Jesus.

It isn't that I never prayed
this before,
but more that I didn't
understand
the power of that ask.
My own fear frenzy

keeps me overfunctioning
and doing my part, your part
maybe even trying to do
God's part.
That's where my confession
begins.

I do far too much
for fear that if I don't,
others won't.
And some days I've placed
God
among those others.

Lord, forgive me.
Help me.
Free me.

Come, Lord Jesus.

Deeper Roots

Over the past several years, I've learned a lot about plants, and
growing things. One of the things that has become clear to
me is that deep roots don't just happen; they are cultivated
with intention. Remember our idea of a *How Things Work*
episode for spiritual life? If your desire is to grow deep spiritual
roots of faith, allow me to name some repeatable patterns of

discipleship that will ground you in the love and person of
Jesus.

There are many books about spiritual formation, and
specifically the disciplines that yield transformation in the
Christian life. For someone who is beginning again, or looking
to reset in their spiritual life, I would encourage a daily Bible
reading plan, prayer using a journal or app to help you stay
consistent, and intentional time in community and in solitude.

Where might you start with a Bible reading plan? Consider
beginning in a gospel: Matthew, Mark, Luke, or John. Read
a small section each day, perhaps one story or passage, and
before you begin, invite the Holy Spirit to reveal something
new to you. Consider reading the passage more than once.
Listen for a word or phrase that rises to the top for you; jot
that down and keep it with you through the day. Return to it
often! Think about it. Ask the Lord to make it real in your life.

When you pray, consider putting pen to paper. This helps in
multiple ways! It helps with focus and concentration. It also
gives you a way to look back on your prayers, and to see God's
faithfulness in answering those petitions. There are so many
different ways to pray. Sometimes I journal in prose form.
Other times I write a piece of poetry. I may record a passage
of Scripture, word for word, as a way of meditating on it. I also
sometimes draw a picture, or a mind-map, or pray in color in
my journal. All of these are ways that work for me. (Later, there
will be a whole chapter on praying through seasons of difficulty,
so stay tuned for much more about prayer! This is just a way to
begin for now.)

Community and solitude are two critical components of the
spiritual life that balance one another.[5] In community, we
benefit from walking alongside others, including the times
when others uplift us and the times when others rub us wrong.
All of this helps us grow spiritually! All of this, including
the "one-anothers" of Scripture, are lived out in a community
of faith. More and more, amid this odd post-pandemic time,
I see people becoming only loosely connected (if at all) to a
community of faith. I encourage you to pick a place and commit
yourself to community, as a spiritual practice that will deepen
your roots.

Just like we need others to grow, we also need time alone to
grow. Solitude is about drawing away; something we see Jesus
doing over and over in Scripture. What is your current pattern
for drawing away? Ideally, you have a daily rhythm for this sort
of time, but there is also great benefit in spending more time
in a regular rhythm, for instance—several hours of time with
Jesus on a monthly basis, to go deeper and pray about what you
see across the spiritual landscape of your life. You may find, as
I often do, that daily time with Jesus doesn't always afford the
chance to go as deep as you desire. Holding space for deeper
places of solitude is a valuable spiritual practice that will help
your roots to grow deep.

Clean
(based on John 13:3-5)

Your heart is cracked open
wide
admirable, the beauty and
humility on display
as You reach for my feet,
searching out the unlovely in
me.

I'd rather show You my
shine,
but Your splendor now
eclipses
ten toes
to show me
that whatever I'd rather
hide
belongs in Your hands,
and I'm astounded to see
You've transformed what I
deemed unworthy,
and prepared me to carry
grace to others
all by washing my unlovely,
making me clean.

1. https://twitter.com/stevecusswords/status/13312338616
28379137/.

2. Grace Hauck, "Americans are using alcohol to cope with pandemic stress: Nearly 1 in 5 report 'heavy drinking'," USA Today, September 22, 2021, https://www.usatoday.com/story/news/health/2021/09/2 2/covid-19-pandemic-heavy-drinking-survey-alkermes/ 5798036001/.

3. Hashir Ali Awan et al., "Internet and Pornography Use During the COVID-19 Pandemic: Presumed Impact and What Can Be Done," Frontiers in Psychiatry, Mary 16, 2021, https://doi.org/10.3389/fpsyt.2021.623508/.

4. Steven Covey, The Seven Habits of Highly Effective People: Powerful Lessons in Personal Change (New York: Simon & Schuster, 1989).

5. Richard Foster, Celebrations of Discipline: The Path to Spiritual Growth (San Francisco: HarperSanFrancisco, 1998), 96–97.

4

IN THE WEEDS

Knots

A simple strand of string can
quickly
become a knot in me,
end turned on end,
intertwined and pulled tight.
But I've learned what to do
with the knots I can't work
through:
I can bring them all to You.
Your hands—big enough to
hold all there is—
are also somehow
perfectly-sized for working
out
delicate jumbles like this.
"Patience," You whisper.

"Don't pull against Me.
Turn it over, let it go—let

the tension release."
For a while, I may wonder if
You'll really sort it out,
then it's done, and I
remember: I should never
doubt.
There is no tangle You
cannot master,
no cord in me You can't set
right.
Working out my disordered
heartstrings
is Your joy and Your delight.
So, restore order in me;
stretch out every strand
again.
I will welcome Your work of
undoing!
Let setting me right begin.

"The seed cast in the weeds represents the ones
who hear the kingdom news but are overwhelmed
with worries about all the things they have to do
and all the things they want to get. The stress
strangles what they heard, and nothing comes of
it." (Mark 4:18-19)

I've heard more people confess worry and fear as a troubling condition in their spiritual life in the last several years than anything else. It usually sounds something like this, "I get stuck in worry. Sometimes I feel so much anxiety over the future, and I don't want to live like that. But I don't know how to let it go." Or "I'm really fearful most of the time. It seems like every decision I'm making carries potentially huge consequences, and I fear getting it wrong." Can you relate?

Unlike some of the patterns we talked about in the last two chapters that can be subtle and hard to name, we are most often quickly able to point out worry or fear as an unwelcome house guest whom we must evict. No one wants to live with worry or fear! The problem isn't naming it, the problem is that we can't quite seem to shake it.

Jesus talks directly about worry and fear—not only in this parable, but in other key passages, too. Here worry is like a weed or a thorn that chokes out the good seed. It occupies space in our heart, and it quickly enlarges to overtake our quarters, seeming to occupy every nook and cranny. It's hard for faith to grow where the wild weeds of worry are multiplying. What do we do about this type of soil?

Disciples are those who are being shaped into the image of Jesus, through the daily apprenticing of His character and love. Part of being a disciple is the rooting out of anything in our lives that shrinks the gospel of Jesus in our lives.[1] When we are living in a spirit of worry or fear, it not only makes our lives smaller (in contrast to the abundant life that Jesus offers), but it also shrinks the gospel in our lives, because our minds are fixated on those worries and fears, rather than the presence and power of Christ.

Be encouraged: we can weed out a lot of this worry and fear! To do so, we must understand some of the common underlying themes that bring these weeds into full form in our lives, as well as the unhealthy human responses that they inevitably trigger and put us at odds with the gospel of Jesus. Once we get a grasp on our fears and how we respond to them, then we can begin to orient ourselves away from them and toward the gospel. Let's get started!

The Role of Pattern Recognition in Spiritual Life

When my kids were little, we saw a brilliant pediatrician whom I'll call Dr. S. She was thorough and took her time in every appointment. Sometimes, when a child presented with one set of symptoms, she asked questions that might have seemed unrelated to that primary set of symptoms, at least to my untrained eye. One day she unpacked this for me.

"Being a good doctor is largely about pattern recognition," Dr. S. explained. "Usually, in medicine, there are patterns that emerge. Doctors learn the patterns, and then recognize them in patients to make accurate diagnosis. The more quickly I can recognize patterns, ruling some out and holding others as possibilities, the more quickly we can have a plan to move forward."

Hence, all the questions about what I thought were unrelated things. Part of her expertise was to recognize how things I thought irrelevant could actually be relevant in understanding the bigger picture and finding the right way forward.

Now, others from the medical community may agree or disagree with Dr. S, but what she offered me that day (besides patient and thorough medical care for our little one) was an insight into my own work as a pastor and Christ-follower. I do some of the same things, but in spiritual life: I try to name, and help others recognize, patterns. Perhaps we could more broadly assert that part of discipleship is recognizing patterns and responding in realignment.

Some Familiar Thought Patterns

So if we were looking for patterns of thought that might fuel worry or fear, what could those be?

A primary pattern that can lead to worry and fear is one that is rooted in control. We talked about the need for control as something that can cause rocky soil; as humans, we're prone to seek control in circumstances more than we seek God, because being in control feels good! When we have a strong desire for control and we feel we're losing that control, worry and fear set in bigtime. To see this pattern, I invite you to list out some of what you're worrying about right now in life.

Now look at your list and evaluate: place a checkmark by everything that you *actually* have control over. (Not influence, not an indirect relationship, but actual control.) I think you'll find that your list is largely composed of the kinds of things we *wish* we could control, but we cannot. The truth is that we control very little, don't we?

Here's the thing: that which we cannot control, we must surrender. If that sounds like it should be easy, don't be fooled. Surrendering what we cannot control is one of the largest works of spiritual discipleship! It is also the work that frees us from this pattern, because a new pattern piece emerges, something called *trust*.

Trust says, "I can't control this at all, God. But Scripture tells me that You hold all things together, and that You work all things for my good. So I'm going to choose trust."

When you're working on patterns in thought life, it can be helpful to have a physical prompt that realigns your heart and reminds you of the pattern-breaking truth. For me, simple index cards do the trick! I keep them with my journaling supplies, and when I discover a truth that I need to hold onto, I write it on an index card. From time to time, I revisit these cards, allowing the truth to sink into my heart and mind. You will probably not be surprised when I tell you that I've got an index card right now in my stack that simply says, "I choose trust."

Another thought pattern that can be problematic is one that doesn't hold space for good and bad to coexist in life.[2] Here's the truth: as much as we'd like things to be "all good" or "all bad," that is a very big oversimplification of life. No one is perfect (except Jesus) and even the strongest people are sometimes weak. Churches fail us, and people disappoint. Jobs don't work out. We think we're well, then we learn there is disease in our body, and we had no idea. Good people can make really poor choices.

When we don't hold space for good and bad to coexist, we are often beside ourselves at the behavior of people, the disappointment of situations, and the general state of the world. From this inability to understand the complexity of humanity (which shows itself, by the way, right from the beginning—when Adam and Eve eat the apple in the garden), we set expectations for ourselves and for others that are unattainable.

First, the inward self-talk of all good or all bad demands that I must be perfect, or I'm not good. For those who are stuck in this pattern of thinking, there's a constant disappointment with self and worry about falling short, not measuring up. There is fear about not meeting the standard of perfection. Here's the thing: perfection is a myth! Steve Cuss says it this way, "You are 100% human-sized." There is simply no escaping this! Looking for perfection is always going to result in fallout.

When we don't hold space for good and bad to coexist, we demand that others be "all good." And when they fail, we don't have a category for it. This creates a different kind of worry and fear; every time a person or situation isn't perfect, we are left reeling with the shortcomings, and what that means for the relationship or circumstance. This can also be an anticipatory anxiety, where we are concerned in advance about how a situation may play out. If you are a parent, this is an especially easy place to let worry and fear take up residence, as catastrophizing the negative leads to even more worry and fear.

Years ago, I experienced a really difficult situation in my career and quickly realized there was a long list of people I'd need to forgive. However, when a friend challenged me to also list the places of gratitude, I was stopped in my tracks. Gratitude? Did she know how I'd been burned?

This is an example of our human desire to categorize. "Make it good, or make it bad, but don't ask me to see both!" But I am (gently) asking you to see both, if you want to work out of this pattern.

False gospels and the Good News

Whatever diminishes the gospel of Jesus in our lives is something we must root out! There is a false gospel at work in the patterns above, and that must be named and dealt with. The false gospel is one of self-reliance. Steve Cuss explains it this way, "When we are under pressure, tired, anxious, or feeling threatened, our tendency is to depend on ourselves rather than on God."[3]

Wow, there is so much truth in this statement! This false gospel of self-reliance is at work in the patterns of control and the inability to hold space for both good and bad. Let me explain.

In both of these patterns, there is a tendency to depend solely on self. When we are seeking control in a situation, it's because we've decided to count on our own ability, rather than anyone else's. If we can direct the outcome, we can bring about the best outcome. This is classic self-reliance. The true gospel tells us that we don't have to control outcomes; Jesus has already determined the final outcome. There is a lot of wide-open space to rest in this truth, and that is His invitation to us: to rest in the work He's already done, not anything we might control, or do.

When we fail to hold space for both good and bad, we rely on our own perfection, or the ability of others to perform and measure up in every situation or circumstance (others-reliance). Again, this puts far too much weight on humans! None of us will always measure up. We will misstep, and we will fail.

The truth of the gospel of Jesus is that Jesus has bought out our mistakes and missteps. That's what redemption means: it's a buying out. He bought our freedom by going to the cross for our sins. If we could be perfect, we wouldn't have needed Jesus to go to the cross. Grace tells us that we can never reach perfection, but also reminds us that we don't have to: Jesus has done this work for us as well.

Posture Check

When Jesus talks about worry, He invites people to consider examples of His great care that are already present around them in the world. Consider the lilies, He says. Notice how they don't toil, but they're clothed in beauty. Consider the sparrows, He invites. Notice how rich their provision is.

As we are working through worry and fear, part of right-sizing these responses lies in changing what we're noticing. So much of what we worry about has to do with circumstances around us. Our list of fears comprises all the "what ifs" of life.

In her devotional classic *Jesus Today,* Sarah Young draws out a difference between glancing and gazing. Keep in mind that she writes from the perspective of Jesus speaking directly to the reader:

> Gaze at Me; glance at
> problems—this is the secret

of living victoriously. Your
tendency is to gaze at
problems for prolonged
periods of time, glancing at
Me for help. This is natural
for someone with a fallen
mind living in a fallen world.
However, I have called you
to live supernaturally, and I
have empowered you to do
so. The Holy Spirit, who
lives in all My followers,
enables you to live beyond
yourself—to transcend your
natural tendencies.[4]

Too often, we only glance at God's promises and where He is at work in the world, while we gaze at our problems. We put our primary focus on circumstances and situations.

Jesus seems to invite us to flip that script. Consider the lilies, consider the sparrows! Look at how God works in the world; don't just glance at it, gaze at it! Turn it over in your mind. Determine to notice God in your daily life.

We've talked about God's part and our part in faith life. One important thing we are accountable for is our spiritual posture. Through the faith posture of noticing,[5] we are invited to learn more and more about God: how He works, where He is moving, and what He is up to.

As we recognize and name the places that God is at work, we begin to right-size fear and worry, holding them up alongside our Great God. Our renewed and intentional focus on God's work in the world also helps to right-size the gospel in our hearts, recognizing the necessity of relying completely on Jesus, who He is, and what He's done for us.

Rehearsing the Promises

I grew up in theater, taking progressively larger roles on the stage over my growing up years. Practicing scenes definitely helps you learn the blocking, the pacing, the interaction that happens on the stage. But nothing substitutes for the work of running lines.

If you really want to learn the call and response of a scene, and to nail the interaction by knowing all your lines, you've got to rehearse those lines until they are second nature. To this day, I can tell you the opening lines of *My Fair Lady,* and I performed in that show several decades ago! (*"Two bunches of violets, trod in the mud. A full day's wages! Why don't you look where you're going?"*)

The same is true of spiritual life. There's a constant call-and-response in a life of faith. We are repeatedly in conversation with others, with situations and circumstances, and with God in prayer. We're also in an internal call-and-response; information comes in, and our responses go back out. To increase your faith, try running some lines to get rooted deeply in godly responses.

We can move through the distressing weeds of worry and fear by shifting our focus onto God's promises, which are laced through the whole of Scripture. Again, I point you to an index card system! When you need to pick up a new way of seeing, you must rehearse it.

Here is a section of Scripture that has helped me in many ways, as I've committed it to memory and rehearsed it in my heart:

> Don't panic. I'm with you. There's no need to fear for I'm your God. I'll give you strength. I'll help you. I'll hold you steady, keep a firm grip on you. (Isa 41:10)

While these words were first spoken to the Israelites, in Christ these words are now spoken to all of us. I find it so helpful to meditate on this verse, phrase by phrase:

"Don't panic. I'm with you." You are never alone! Wherever you are, whatever you are facing, God is with you. He hems you in, before and behind. Everything difficult is easier to face with a partner; God is the most capable and faithful One you will ever know. He has promised His presence, so you can count on it. Rehearse this promise.

"There's no need to fear for I'm your God." Our God defines Himself in Scripture with these words, "I Am that I Am" (Exod. 3:14). God is constantly revealing His character and heart to people across the pages of Scripture, and to you and me, as well. In Genesis 15, God tells Abram, I am your Shield." The "I am" statements of Jesus help us to understand much more deeply this God who is with us: He is the Way, the Truth, and the Life, the Door, the Vine, the Resurrection and the Life, the Light of the World, the Bread of Life, the Alpha and Omega, the First and Last. Wherever you are and whatever you are facing, consider finding a name of God that speaks to your specific need, and to praise God for that aspect of His character, which has been revealed and is being revealed now in your life. He is your God! Rehearse the promise found in the name that reveals His character.

"I'll give you strength." God helps us to be strong, alert, courageous, brave and bold! Remember the Source of your strength. None of us is strong apart from God; God gives us strength.

"I'll help you." Knowing that God is with us is amazing, isn't it? But then this: God isn't just here; He is here *to help*. Let's take that in for a moment and really sit with this truth. There are all sorts of people who come and go from our lives —some are helpers and some, well, not so much. God is One who comes and stays, and He helps *always*. This is a promise we can rest in and rehearse.

"I'll hold you steady, keep a firm grip on you." I don't know about you, but when I feel like I'm on unsteady ground, One who can keep me upright is what I'm looking for. Look no further than God—His righteous right hand is on your life, and He is holding you when you need it most. In Scripture, God's right hand is an instrument of blessing and of deliverance. The fact that God holds us steady reminds us of His intimate presence in our lives.

Rehearsing these promises, and others like this, builds our strength. It helps to right-size the gospel in our lives, returning our focus to the ever-present truth of God's character and person. Time spent memorizing Scripture will reap dividends in your spiritual life; these words will flood back to you when you need them most. This has happened in my own life over and over again; I know it will also be true for you. Consider spending a week steeping in the promises of Isaiah 41:10, one promise per day, for a shift in perspective in your spiritual life.

Rhythms and Community

Often when our lives are filled with worry and fear, we are prone to withdraw. Moving away from others feels more comfortable when we are struggling deeply with anxious thoughts. But community is so important in times like these: we don't beat worry and fear in isolation. Knowing that others are with us, even pulling for us when we feel we're losing ground, helps us to find strength to move forward.

Daily rhythms are also very important in helping us get out of patterns that produce worry and fear. For instance, when was the last time you took a walk or did something physical? What did you eat today? Yesterday? Over the past week? And how much are you sleeping right now? The answers to these questions are important in your overall health and well-being, but especially when you feel your life is riddled with worry and fear. Examine these rhythms as patterns, too, and seek to make small changes that will move you to greater health in your daily life.

One last reminder: counseling is one of the healthiest decisions you can ever make! If you find yourself stuck in worry and fear, I encourage you to seek out the help of a professional who can walk with you through this season. Maybe today's goal can be to make that appointment; you will be glad that you did.

Today

Today, be brave.
We all feel fear;
bravery is choosing
not to be that fear.

So, don't rehearse
the worry.
Choose not to act
out of anxiety.

Instead, pick
another to embody:
choose to be Love.

Love sends fear packing,
throws fear's belongings
out onto the street
and locks the door tight.

Yes, today, be brave,
and let love lead.

1. Steve Cuss, Managing Leadership Anxiety: Yours and Theirs (Nashville: Thomas Nelson, 2019), 19.

2. For more on this, read chapters 12 and 13 of Henry Cloud, Changes That Heal: The Four Shifts That Make Everything Better—and That Anyone Can Do (Grand Rapids, MI: Zondervan, 1990).. He breaks this down with great detail, and his work in this area is very insightful.

3. Cuss, Managing Leadership Anxiety, 12.

4. Sarah Young, Jesus Today: Experience Hope Through His Presence (Nashville: Thomas Nelson, 2012), 58.

5. Holly Sprink, Faith Postures: Cultivating Christian Mindfulness (Macon, GA: Smyth & Helwys, 2009). 8.

5

—— • ——

HARD GROUND

The Desperate Woman
(based on Mark 5:25-34)

Today I'm her
pushing through the people
to reach for a piece of You
Desperate to find You
and receive healing,
no matter what the risk.

Some days I wish I was You,
able to heal, able to speak
performative words
over broken hearts and
bodies and minds,

But I'm no savior.
I'm just the one trying
to find answers,
to be healed,

to be whole,
to hear You call me daughter.

Maybe I thought I was
pushing through for others,
but the whole truth is - I'm
her.

The poetry you just read is based on a story in Mark about a
woman who is pretty desperate to be healed. Scripture tells
us that this woman has been bleeding for twelve years. Twelve
years! Is that even possible? To never stop bleeding for twelve
years? Wouldn't you become anemic and terribly faint? (I
digress.)

But this is her reality, and that isn't all. She's on the outskirts
of every part of life, living beyond the city gates. This is
because women who were bleeding in biblical times were
considered unclean and forced to vacate their home, go to
the outside of the city gates, and await the stop of their
cycle before returning. Imagine waking up every day to see
more blood—for twelve whole years? Did she build a house or
structure outside of the walls? Maybe so. But probably not,
because she was also broke.

That's right, the passage tells us she has spent all of her money
on treatments, but none of them worked. So she's pressing
in to try to see Jesus as this story unfolds in Mark's gospel.
She must believe Jesus to be the Messiah, because in the story,

she's reaching for the hem of his garment, or the wings—the Tzitzit.[1]

We don't talk about this part of the story often, about how she's reaching for the hem of Jesus's garment. It isn't that she thinks she just needs to touch the edge of his garment; I believe she's purposefully reaching for healing. I believe she's got this verse that is found in Mal. 4:2 in her mind, which says, "But for you who revere my name the sun of righteousness shall rise, with healing in its wings. You shall go out leaping like calves from the stall" (NRSV).

Healing in what wings, you may ask? Well, quite literally in Jewish tradition, the four corners of Jesus' cloak, the Tzitzit, would also be called the wings of the garment. Believing that Jesus fulfills prophecy, she is boldly reaching for his Tzitzit. And as she grabs hold of the wing of his garment, something miraculous happens: this woman, who has bled for twelve straight years, receives healing! The bleeding stops, and her physical health is restored.

But the story doesn't end there:

> At the same moment, Jesus felt energy discharging from him. He turned around to the crowd and asked, "Who touched my robe?"
> His disciples said, "What are you talking about? With this crowd pushing and jostling you, you're asking, 'Who touched me?' Dozens have touched you!"
> But he went on asking, looking around to see who had done it. The woman, knowing what had

happened, knowing she was the one, stepped up
in fear and trembling, knelt before him, and gave
him the whole story.
Jesus said to her, "Daughter, you took a risk of
faith, and now you're healed and whole. Live well,
live blessed! Be healed of your plague." (Mark
5:30-34)

This is one of my favorite stories in Scripture, because Jesus
doesn't leave the woman with a sneaky healing. He knows
someone has been healed, and he wants to talk to them. "Who
touched my robe?" isn't an accusatory question, but rather an
invitation.

Let's be clear: Jesus knows all things. He is fully God,
remember? This means he is already aware of who has touched
his robe. Like so many of Jesus's questions throughout the
pages of Scripture, the question is for the woman's benefit, not
his.

Tell me who you are, Jesus implores. Let me hear your story.
And so the woman comes forward, kneels, and gives him "the
whole story." She speaks the whole truth to Jesus, and as a
result she emerges not only healed, but whole.

Sometimes we struggle to tell Jesus the whole story. It is
messy—and hard. We're not always proud of what we feel and
why. But gaining freedom from the hardest ground in our lives
requires that we name the place and the feelings and that we
tell Jesus the whole truth. The truth, after all, is what sets us
free. Here's an excerpt of what it looks like to tell the whole
truth from my journal:

THERE WAS A LOT OF SCRIBBLING, SCRAWLING AND
MADNESS YESTERDAY . . . AND THEN A RIPPED-OUT
PAGE FROM MY JOURNAL. I BALLED IT UP AND THREW
IT AWAY. HOW I WISH I COULD DO THAT WITH THE
ANGER AND SADNESS I FEEL. I FINALLY NAMED IT:
GRIEF. I'VE LOST MYSELF.

THERE IT IS, GOD, THAT'S THE WHOLE TRUTH.
AND THERE IS FEAR THAT I WON'T FIND "ME"
AGAIN—SO I'M FEELING PRETTY DESPERATE. I DON'T
KNOW THE NEXT THING TO DO, SO I KEEP PUSHING
THROUGH—TRYING TO FIND YOU. PLEASE HELP
ME—TO SOMEHOW FIND MY WAY AGAIN. ALSO, HELP
ME TO KEEP HONORING YOU. I'M STRUGGLING HARD,
GOD. AMEN.

Hard ground has lots of names: anger, grief, jealousy,
heartache, desolation, disappointment, envy, and resentment
are a few of the emotions that come to mind that might need
to be plowed up, and the soil turned over, for healing to begin.

Recently, I sat with friends and we talked about some hard
ground. One friend confessed, "Pray for my anger. I don't know
why I feel it; it seems to come from nowhere. I know it isn't
good, and I don't know what to do with it." Another added, "I
just feel so disappointed with where I am right now. My work
doesn't even feel fulfilling any more. It's just something I have
to do every day." Each time these words are spoken, each time
confessions are made, heads bob up and down in agreement.
This isn't just one person's struggle—this is every person's

struggle. One person has had the courage to speak it, and that allows each of us around the circle to own it.

If you are feeling some of the more difficult emotions in life, you are not alone. In fact, I think you are in very good company. Most importantly, Jesus invites you into His company, hard emotions in tow, where He can help you to unpack those emotions, till the soil of hard ground, and move forward in faith. This is vital work, because hard ground keeps us from receiving the seed that is being sown into our lives. Remember Jesus's words? "The farmer plants the Word. Some people are like the seed that falls on the hardened soil of the road. No sooner do they hear the Word than Satan snatches away what has been planted in them" (Mark 4:14-15). So if you are in a place of hard ground, this type of soil must be addressed.

Some Guiding Principles for Hard Emotions

There are four guiding principles I offer you, as a theological framework through which we can look at and understand hard ground:

1. God gave humans emotions; He created all of the emotions we feel.

2. God intended you to move through the emotions that cause hard ground. When you get stuck in them, you can get stuck in life, too. If you are finding yourself there, you may need help to move forward.

3. Emotions are real *and* not every emotion you feel is grounded in truth. Sometimes hard emotions are grounded in lies, and those faulty ways of thinking

must be rooted out for you to move forward.

4. True emotions are like signal lights in a car; they
   are symptoms of what is happening in your soul. You
   move through them by embracing the hard ground and
   working with God to till the soil of your heart. That
   work involves telling God the whole truth, and owning
   your experience with Him, in a way that you maybe
   haven't before.

There is hope when you find you're at a place of difficult
emotions that seem to be ruling your life. There is a way to
bring them back under control, and submit them daily to God,
so you don't have to live from these feelings. Ready to get to
work?

Jesus explains this parable to his disciples, and what he tells
them about the hard ground stops me in my tracks:

> "The farmer plants the Word. Some people are
> like the seed that falls on the hardened soil of the
> road. No sooner do they hear the Word than Satan
> snatches away what has been planted in them."
> (Mark 4:14-15)

Did you get that? The seed that falls on the hard ground is
never received; it simply gets snatched away shortly after it is
released onto the hard ground. So, if you are resonating with
this type of soil, you may recognize as you are reading this that,
when you are exposed to faith, or the truth of Scripture, or
anything that might help your spiritual life to grow, it doesn't

seem to truly get into the soil of your heart. Many people find themselves here at this point in time. What do we do about this?

The first step to navigating hard ground is to figure out where you are struggling. Do not say, "Everywhere!" (Don't freak out, either, like "how did she know that?" I can read your mind, because *I am you*.) But "everywhere" is too vague as a place to start. It is easier to name an emotion from a list than to pull an emotion out of thin air, so I'm offering up some vocabulary of emotions, from the work of Marshall Rosenberg, PhD, to help you put your finger on the one(s) you are feeling:

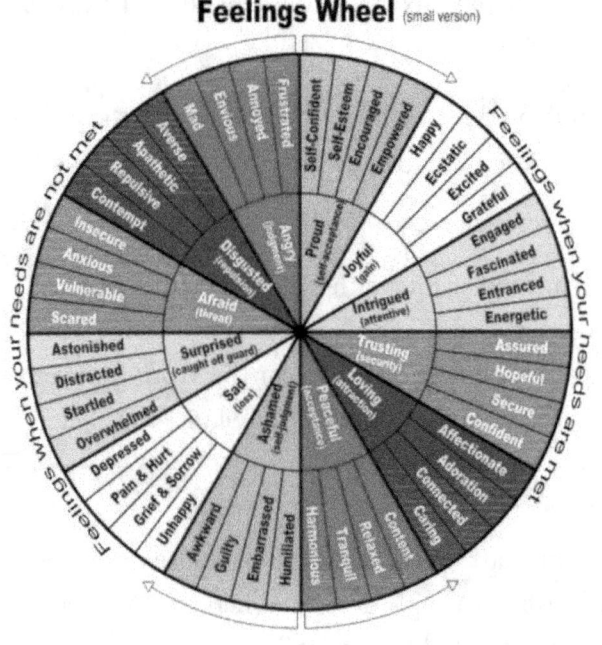

2

Spend a minute studying this image. As you linger here; what do you see?

What rises to the top for me is that there are so many feelings
we often don't name. These feelings connect to feelings we
often name, like being angry, sad, or afraid; I call the feelings
we name easily and often our "frequent-flier feelings." But the
more detailed we can be in naming the internal emotions we
are feeling, the easier it is to bring those to Jesus's feet and tell
the whole truth.

Because emotions like these are signals, not the root cause
of our pain, we must name them in order to tame them.[3]
When we are putting off sirens as we move through the
day—whether those sirens are emotions like anger that boils
over quickly or fear that sounds off to let the room know that all
is not well—identifying the emotion is the first step in moving
forward.

Once we've come up with a list of the emotions, the next
question is, what is behind that emotion? Why am I feeling
angry? What is causing the grief that is showing up for me?
Why was I embarrassed in that interaction? What is the root
of my anxiety? What am I afraid will happen? I recommend
when you start to sort out emotions, you use a journal as a
processing tool. There is not a wrong answer! We're looking
to uncover what is under the emotion, not to judge what is
under the emotion. We aren't there yet! Suspend judgment
about everything you write down; just get it out.

Do you have that list? If not, I urge you to really write this all
down. Writing helps us right our hearts and minds! If you don't
believe me, try it. All you've got to lose is a little ink and a few
minutes. Once you've got a list, it may help you to sleep on it,
and then revisit it once more the following day.

Read your writing—and read it *slowly*. Sit with it; hold it in God's light. Is what you've written the whole truth? Is there anything else you need to add?

Permission to read your mind? I feel like you might be thinking: Christy, if I write it all down, I will surely wear God out! He doesn't want to hear all of this!!

Let me answer you boldly, and tell you what I think Jesus might say:

> *Oh, but beloved child, I do.*
> *I want to hear every last bit*
> *of it.*
> *Get it out—it is good for*
> *you to get it out.*
> *Bring it straight to me, so I*
> *can help you sort through*
> *it.*
> *Come to Me when you feel*
> *weary and burdened—and*
> *let Me give you rest.*

God can't be exhausted by you. You want to know why? Because God is indefatigable.

Now, as you hold this work of naming the hard ground in God's presence, let's ask for the Spirit's help: "Search me, O God, and know my heart. Test me, and know my anxious thoughts." Or, in Eugene Peterson's translation:

Investigate my life, O God,
find out everything about me;
Cross-examine and test me,
get a clear picture of what I'm about;
See for yourself whether I've done anything
wrong—
then guide me on the road to eternal life.
(Ps. 139:23)

Here are a few prayer prompts to help you hold your journaling
in God's light:

Holy Spirit, what is true?

Show me the places I'm being deceived right now.

Illuminate the faulty thinking; I know I am prone to faulty
thinking. Show me, God.

That's like a modern day, "Search my heart."

What is True?

You may be wondering, don't I decide my own truth?

I'm so glad you asked.

Your emotions are real, I don't question for a moment that
you feel this way. But feelings follow thinking, and thinking
can get confused. It's possible to build our thinking on faulty
ground, and it gets even trickier: once we become committed to
a thought pattern, our mind seeks to prove it. In other words,
we look for evidence of what we've come to believe, and we may

cast aside other messages—even true ones—if they don't fit the lens we've picked up in any given area.

So our emotions must be held in the light of God's truth and love—and we must ask His help in discerning what is true.

When you've whittled your list to the true emotions—for instance, you feel grief over a loss, angry at being downsized, or you are struggling with feeling unseen and unappreciated—when you've gotten to those true emotions, it is time to lament.

The Power of Lament

Lamenting is almost a lost art in Christian community, but it is biblical, and it is so important! Why else would the psalms be filled with lament?

What is a lament, you may be wondering? A lament is when you cry out to God about something, when you raise a complaint to Him. In the Bible, there are both corporate and individual laments. Corporate laments address concerns of the community—for instance, we might offer a corporate lament about racial inequity, or war, or crime in the streets, or food insecurity. These are things we can all point to, and we wonder (if we are honest) where is God in this? We link arms with others and cry out, complaining about what we see and imploring God to move.

Individual laments are the prayers of people over their personal situations. These are super-honest, bold prayers with a few components. They offer a complaint or grievance to God and point out God's perceived relative absence in this situation. They lament the hardship of the situation, with specifics. And

then, at some point, inevitably, they turn toward a statement
of faith in how God will indeed show up, and they are counting
on it.

Let's use Psalm 22 (a psalm of individual lament) as an
example, so we can break down the anatomy of a lament. The
psalmist begins pouring out their heart to God, confessing how
hard life is, and how disappointed they are by God's seeming
absence and indifference.

> God, God . . . my God!
> Why did you dump me
> miles from nowhere?
> Doubled up with pain, I call to God
> all the day long. No answer. Nothing.
> I keep at it all night, tossing and turning.
> And you! Are you indifferent, above it all,
> leaning back on the cushions of Israel's praise?
> We know you were there for our parents:
> they cried for your help and you gave it;
> they trusted and lived a good life.
> And here I am, a nothing—an earthworm,
> something to step on, to squash.
> Everyone pokes fun at me;
> they make faces at me, they shake their heads:
> "Let's see how God handles this one;
> since God likes him so much, let him help him!"
> And to think you were midwife at my birth,
> setting me at my mother's breasts!
> When I left the womb you cradled me;
> since the moment of birth you've been my God.

Then you moved far away
and trouble moved in next door.
I need a neighbor.
Herds of bulls come at me,
the raging bulls stampede,
Horns lowered, nostrils flaring,
like a herd of buffalo on the move.
I'm a bucket kicked over and spilled,
every joint in my body has been pulled apart.
My heart is a blob
of melted wax in my gut.
I'm dry as a bone,my tongue black and swollen.
They have laid me out for burial
in the dirt.
Now packs of wild dogs come at me;
thugs gang up on me.
They pin me down hand and foot,
and lock me in a cage—a bag
Of bones in a cage, stared at
by every passerby.
They take my wallet and the shirt off my back,
and then throw dice for my clothes. (Ps. 22:1-18)

Note the honesty and clarity of these words, the detailed
imagery of this prayer. The psalmist feels dumped! They call
out to God, but there is no answer. While God was faithful
to prior generations, this psalmist reports that they need a
neighbor. They're attacked and they're like a bucket that's
been kicked and spilled. This is about as specific as it gets, and
the brutal honesty shows us that nothing is off limits in our
prayer life with God.

Next comes a major cry for help, a direct request for God to act—without delay:

> You, God—don't put off my rescue!
> Hurry and help me!
> Don't let them cut my throat;
> don't let those mongrels devour me.
> If you don't show up soon,
> I'm done for—gored by the bulls,
> meat for the lions. (Ps. 22:19-21)

The psalmist seems to order God's help, urgently imploring His presence. "Show up!" the psalmist reels. Lastly, the turn toward God's power to do this thing, and God's power to do anything. Note the total sense of a U-turn in the prayer, as well as the confidence with which the psalmist speaks:

> Here's the story I'll tell my friends when they
> come to worship,
> and punctuate it with Hallelujahs:
> Shout Hallelujah, you God-worshipers;
> give glory, you sons of Jacob;
> adore him, you daughters of Israel.
> He has never let you down,
> never looked the other way
> when you were being kicked around.
> He has never wandered off to do his own thing;
> he has been right there, listening.
> Here in this great gathering for worship

I have discovered this praise-life.
And I'll do what I promised right here
in front of the God-worshipers.
Down-and-outers sit at God's table
and eat their fill.
Everyone on the hunt for God
is here, praising him.
"Live it up, from head to toe.
Don't ever quit!"
From the four corners of the earth
people are coming to their senses,
are running back to God.
Long-lost families
are falling on their faces before him.
God has taken charge;
from now on he has the last word.
All the power-mongers are before him
—worshiping!
All the poor and powerless, too
—worshiping!
Along with those who never got it together
—worshiping!
Our children and their children
will get in on this
As the word is passed along
from parent to child.
Babies not yet conceived
will hear the good news—
that God does what he says. (Ps. 22:22-31)

I particularly love verse 29. The powerful are worshiping. So are the poor and powerless. But the last third of this verse: those who never got it together—they worship, too. You see, no matter where we are on the spectrum, we wind up worshiping in this lament.

If you've never penned a lament, I believe this is one of the most freeing and powerful ways you can pray! By the way, the whole book of Lamentations is—you guessed it—one big lament, as well. If you need to see more examples before you engage your own pen and paper, you can look at other individual psalms of lament like Psalms 3, 6, 31, 44, 56, 57, 77, or 86. (And there are more, but these are good places to begin.)

If you're still wondering whether you can really speak like this to God, I want to point you toward a very powerful example. Jesus, on the cross, quoted the very psalm we used as an example: "My God, my God, why have You forsaken me?" is the opening line of Psalm 22 in most common translations. In the height of His suffering, when anguish had mounted, Jesus quotes the psalmist and laments. If lamenting is good for Jesus, lamenting is good for you and for me.

—————

A Lament, circa 2018

So many closed doors in here
and did I mention, I'm
feeling claustrophobic?

Isn't this where You throw
open a window?
But the windows are
shuttered and we are stuck.
Stuck in a small place,
stuck with a big problem,
stuck in our smallness.

I do not mean to call You
small,
but why aren't You bigger
right now?

When answers do not come
and language fails,
when cries seem insufficient
and tears fall freely
but there are not solutions,
no one is listening to us.

Are you hearing me, God?
Will you answer us, Lord?
Time is ticking away, and
trust is wearing thin.
Please, oh please God,
thicken this skin!

Part the waters
and make a way,
drive back these waves,
make them obey.

You formed this child,
stitched them in my womb.
Now we need healing
that can only come from You.

Do it for them, do it for me.
Do it because of Your
reputation and glory!
But please—please—please
move.
Oh, how we need You.
Show up strongly on our
behalf,
our hope is in You, God—
do not let us be put to shame.

Amen.

In a way that I cannot explain, but you can only
experience-to-know, lamenting helps us as humans to turn the
corner on difficult emotions. It helps us to till the soil of hard
ground, maybe like nothing else.

Counseling helps! Good conversations with trusted friends and
loved ones, those help, too. But naming the heartache and
holding it up to God—telling Him the whole truth—that helps
like nothing else, in my experience.

Coming Full Circle

What did the woman who was healed of her bleeding stand to gain by turning back and owning her experience before Jesus? She gained what might be the most precious thing of all: Jesus gives her a new identity. She came as a commoner, maybe even an outsider. But after she interacts with Jesus and lays the truth bare, He calls her daughter.

When a body is healed of pain and disease, that is a tremendous gift. But the gift of an identity as a daughter or son of the King? That, my friend, is priceless. That is one thing that changes everything. Till up the hard ground and offer that truth to Jesus. His unconditional love is ready to hear your pain and help you find healing, and hope, and identity beyond what you ever imagined was possible.

It's your turn: go ahead and tell Jesus why you've reached for His hem. Tell Him where you need healing. Tell Him the whole truth! No holding back. If you're having trouble getting started, consider borrowing these words from the psalmist: "I'm hurt and in pain; Give me space for healing, and mountain air" (Ps. 69:26). Using that as your first line, let loose and bring the truth straight to Jesus. He can handle it.

~ele~

The Double-Bonus

Declare a double-bonus,

God!
Everything we lost, returned
twice.
That's Your way, God!
Yes, that's Your style.

You do not only redeem and
restore,
You overflow.

I cannot predict how You will
work,
but I do know with certainty
that You are working.

So, rebuild it better, God:
A double-bonus following
the difficult,
a God-sized return on our
frailty and inadequacy.
Amen.

---

1. https://servantofmessiah.org/hebraic-biblical-studies/he
   aling-hem/.
2. Marshall Rosenberg, Nonviolent Communication: A
   Language of Life (Los Angeles: Puddledancer, 2015).
3. Cuss, Managing Leadership Anxiety, 18.

6

GOOD GROUND

Apprenticing

I am apprenticing
for a way of life
I couldn't have dreamed
for impact that will surely
exceed
my limited human capacity.

This is discipleship:
Showing up to be re-formed
again and again
mindful that my reshaping is
never done
leaning in, moist clay to be
molded by the One
whom I desire in likeness to
become.

I am apprenticing.

We've considered three kinds of soil that are problematic in spiritual life. What, then, happens in the good ground? Jesus says it this way:

> "But the seed planted in the good earth represents
> those who hear the Word, embrace it, and produce
> a harvest beyond their wildest dreams."
> (Mark 4:20)

Good soil receives and embraces the Word. New life springs up! Good things grow. There is ultimately fruit that is evidence of the seed that's been sown and received by the good ground of a fertile heart.

Here another agricultural metaphor in Scripture helps us to flesh out what it looks like to live in this way. Let's look at John, chapter 15:

> I am the Real Vine and my Father is the Farmer.
> He cuts off every branch of me that doesn't bear
> grapes. And every branch that is grape-bearing
> he prunes back so it will bear even more. You are
> already pruned back by the message I have spoken.
>
> Live in me. Make your home in me just as I do
> in you. In the same way that a branch can't bear
> grapes by itself but only by being joined to the

vine, you can't bear fruit unless you are joined with
me.

I am the Vine, you are the branches. When
you're joined with me and I with you, the relation
intimate and organic, the harvest is sure to be
abundant. Separated, you can't produce a thing.
Anyone who separates from me is deadwood,
gathered up and thrown on the bonfire. But if you
make yourselves at home with me and my words
are at home in you, you can be sure that whatever
you ask will be listened to and acted upon. This
is how my Father shows who he is—when you
produce grapes, when you mature as my disciples.

I've loved you the way my Father has loved me.
Make yourselves at home in my love. If you keep
my commands, you'll remain intimately at home in
my love. That's what I've done—kept my Father's
commands and made myself at home in his love.
(John 15:1-10)

In the next section of this book, we will talk more about
pruning; there is so much to say about it. But, here, I want to
focus on this idea of remaining, or being at home in the love
of Jesus. Other translations repeatedly use the word *abide* to
describe this action. Consider just seven of these verses in the
NRSV translation to see this repetition:

"*Abide* in me as I *abide* in you. Just as the branch
cannot bear fruit by itself unless it abides in the
vine, neither can you unless you *abide* in me. I am
the vine, you are the branches. Those who *abide*
in me and I in them bear much fruit, because apart
from me you can do nothing. Whoever does not
abide in me is thrown away like a branch and
withers; such branches are gathered, thrown into
the fire, and burned. If you *abide* in me, and my
words abide in you, ask for whatever you wish,
and it will be done for you. My Father is glorified
by this, that you bear much fruit and become[c]
my disciples. As the Father has loved me, so I
have loved you; *abide* in my love. If you keep my
commandments, you will *abide* in my love, just as
I have kept my Father's commandments and *abide*
in his love." (John 15:4-10, NRSV, italics added)

If you're counting, the word abide just showed up nine times
in seven verses. This sort of repetition on Jesus's part is really
significant! Let's take a minute to understand what Jesus is
inviting us to, as He repeatedly exhorts us to abide.

Abiding is Intimate

"Make your home in Me," Peterson's translation says. This is
a very good way of understanding abiding. Abiding is taking
up an address in something and choosing to live there; it is
choosing to operate from that home base. It is a permanent
residence, not a renting relationship. This is what you feel
when you find your dream home and purchase it. A feeling
floods your heart as you relish the "forever home" that you've

found. That's what abiding feels like: it is the understanding that you're here to stay, because it doesn't get any better than this. Have you come to that place yet spiritually? And if so, are you still living there?

Jesus invites us to take up permanent residence in Him, and He in us. It's a mutual indwelling. But what would that sort of relationship look like? It's hard for our minds to fully understand, but that is for good reason.

Abiding is a Divine-Human Concept

One reason we have difficulty conceptualizing this mutual indwelling is because it is impossible for two humans to truly abide together. Even in our most intimate relationships, we aren't living out this sense of a permanent residence *within* another, where the other is also within us. We cannot—humans cannot do this in our embodied relationships. Marriage is our closest example, but even when we are at home in one another's presence, we don't carry around the other person in the same way that we are built to carry Christ. We can only abide with God.

Since we do not experience the true state of abiding with other human beings, an analogy helps us to further grasp this somewhat abstract concept more deeply. Imagine a large pitcher of water and a sponge. If I submerge the sponge fully into that pitcher of water and leave it there for a moment, I could ask you two questions:

Is the sponge in the water? You would assert that yes, the sponge is in the water. This part is easy to see. It is submerged! It's definitely in the water!

Now is the water in the sponge? Again, the answer is yes, the water is in the sponge. If you want proof that the water is in the sponge, if I lift the sponge from the water and squeeze it, the saturated sponge will drip out water in a stream.

This is what truly abiding looks like: we are like the sponge—and when we abide, we are submerged in the Living Water of Christ. As we take up residence in this Living Water, we soak up His character and promises in such a way that, when we are squeezed (and we will be!), those are the things that come out of us. It's a mutual indwelling that is divine–human; we are in Christ, and He is also in us. That's what abiding looks like. The sponge is soft and pliable; soaking up the Source and releasing it when squeezed.

When Spiritual Life is Like a Dry Sponge

If I pull the same sponge out of the water and leave it apart from that water, it will quickly dry out and become hard—even somewhat brittle. And if I submerge it again in water, it will eventually receive that water. Initially, however, it may seem a little resistant. (Ever run water over a totally dry sponge and watch it flow off the top and sides for a moment?)

For many of us, when difficulty comes in our lives, we tend to withdraw from the Living Water, focusing less on spending time with God, and more on the problems around us and how we might spring into action to fix those problems ourselves. At that point, it doesn't take long to dry out spiritually, even becoming hardened and somewhat brittle.

I have a confession to make: I'm not much of a swimmer. Although I can move across the surface of the deep end of

any pool, I never really submerge my head under the water. I
know, some of you are thinking right now: this is ridiculous.
My family thinks so, too. I am married to a man who swims in
open water like rivers and oceans for fun. My daughter swims
year-round; her strokes are beautiful, and her form is amazing.
What I do in the water as I semi-glide across the top with my
head raised in an awkward position is completely different from
what the rest of my family does at the pool.

To further differentiate myself, I often go to the pool and don't
even get in. It just feels like a lot of work to get wet, if I'm
honest. Because I'm not really a swimmer in any way, I feel out
of my element in the water. So I just hang out by the side, and
occasionally dip into the shallow water to cool down, if it is a
really hot day.

Sometimes I wonder about what it would be like to love the
water. I have thought of taking swimming lessons, so I can
master the art of blowing bubbles and join my family in
relishing the full experience. But I've still never taken the next
step—so for now, I will just lounge by the side of the pool,
watching others take in the complete adventure.

My approach to the pool is not unlike how many of us think
about submerging in the water of Christ. It seems like a
lot of work. We're embarrassed that we don't know all the
right spiritual strokes to really submerge ourselves in it. Or
perhaps, like my poolside experience, we've become content
with the occasional dip into Living Water, which provides
some temporary sense of a fuller spiritual life, but without the
commitment of taking the full plunge.

If your spiritual life feels a lot like a dry sponge right now, I have some excellent news for you: the Living Water is always inviting us to come and abide. We've got a standing invitation to receive in this way, and nothing—not yesterday's, or last month's, or the past decade's, or even a lifetime's dry state—disqualifies us from submerging now.

Getting Into the Living Water

In my own life, I've found that true abiding takes two primary forms. First, there is a drawing away to spend time with Jesus, and then there is a moment-by-moment surrender and awareness of His presence throughout the day. Let's begin with the drawing away.

Jesus models this for us repeatedly in Scripture. He gets up early to go and pray. He withdraws from the crowd to be alone with God. His disciples are looking for Jesus, and they find Him praying. It is a completely consistent pattern for Jesus. This sort of withdrawing should also be a pattern, then, for us!

This begins with setting aside a time and a place to meet with God. I find it is really helpful to designate both a time and place, as it increases consistency in the rhythm of withdrawing. For me, there is a chair in a distraction-free room, where I've taken over the corner of a bookshelf for my own study materials and a journal. I also have colored pens, and index cards, of course! Having the supplies on hand helps me tremendously when I sit down to spend time with Jesus.

Ideally, your withdrawing time includes both Bible reading and prayer; both components are vitally important to keeping good ground, spiritually. When you are approaching the Bible,

it's important to pick a translation that you can read and
understand. It's also crucial to have a plan for reading so you
aren't just doing the "flop and drop" method each morning of
letting the Bible randomly open to a page and dropping your
hand onto a text. Having a pattern for reading ensures that
you are working through different passages, which enables
you to experience a broader reading of Scripture as well.
(I've included a section in the back of this book highlighting
different reading plans I've enjoyed over the years, as well as
some information on prominent translations. So if you are new
at this sort of reading, please take a look there for resources to
help you begin!)

When it comes to prayer, I like to use a journal or to capture
my prayer on paper. There is an entire chapter about prayer
in section two, and it gives you many ideas for ways to pray
that help increase your focus. Prayer becomes both a centering
place as you begin your day and a home base as you return to
prayer throughout the day.

In addition to withdrawing, there is a moment-by-moment
realigning that helps us to continually abide. No decision is
too small to bring before Jesus, and throughout the day, you
can pray to be more aware of His presence, and to feel a deeper
sense of His peace. You can pray to embody Jesus's love, or His
gentleness.

In a very real way, what we pray about reveals our theology.
Theology can be thought of as the set of beliefs we hold about
who God is and how He is at work in the world. So if you believe
that God is at work in the details of your life, you offer those
details up in prayer. If you believe God orders world events

and brings leaders into being, those are things you pray about. What we choose to hold before God shows us what we think He is capable of impacting.

You may read this and feel a little defensive: *Wait, I think God does all those things! I just don't pray about them regularly,* you may think. To this line of thought, I'd offer that if you believe that God can impact something in your life and you need to see His hand at work, then you offer it in prayer. (Perhaps you struggle with knowing how to offer it in prayer! Don't forget to read the chapter on prayer in the next section. It will help you with this by providing some concrete examples to consider.)

Kairos Moments

Another way that God is at work in the world, which helps us to keep good ground in the soil of our hearts, is that He repeatedly reveals His will and ways to us and provides the opportunity to respond in the form of repentance and realignment. Although this prompting is constantly happening in our spiritual lives, we often are too busy or distracted to heed the invitation to turn and go in another direction. How do these moments unfold in our lives, and what should we look for?

Perhaps you've experienced this: you are in the midst of a daily moment and suddenly it seems to slow down or come into a sharper focus for you. The same events are happening, but you are aware of them in a different way. Maybe it is when you are in an argument and suddenly you hear your own words in a different way altogether. Or perhaps it is when you sit down to a meal, and suddenly feel immense gratitude for the plate before you, tasting the flavors in a way you've not tasted them before. Maybe it is in the warmth of a relationship with your child, where time seems to slow down as you notice how quickly they are growing and how they look older than yesterday.

Moments like these can be named as Kairos moments: these are moments when the conditions are right for a change. You're being invited, in these moments, to notice and respond: in the argument, you are noticing how the weight of your own words hits another, and you are invited to engage in righteous anger in a productive way, speaking with respect. Maybe that's not been the tone of what you've been saying; the sudden awareness of this is the Spirit's invitation to stop, repent (turn away and go in another direction), and experience change that realigns you with God's heart in the moment.

In a similar way, gratitude for the plate of food before you may be about simply slowing down to acknowledge God's provision more in your life, or the person who prepared that plate, or the chance to enjoy such a meal when many have no food before them. As you pause to engage this moment, the Lord redirects the attitude of your heart and helps you to realign your course with His will.

It is similar with the sudden awareness of the growth of your child. Time seems to slow, giving you the chance to realize that, in fact, time keeps moving. How are you using the time you have? This is an opportunity to spend a moment with Jesus, reflecting on your long days and short years of parenting; an opportunity to make changes, if needed, to become more like Jesus.

The problem for many of us, spiritually, is that we can acknowledge the Kairos moments, but we don't take the time to evaluate them. This is like receiving an invitation via postal mail to an event. You run your hands over the envelope and then set it aside, forgetting all about it and missing the invite and then the event. We must open our spiritual mail, and we must be present to the Kairos moments that are inviting us to change.

The Kairos Learning Circle

There are six steps to moving through the circle of evaluated experience, repentance, and belief, when we recognize a Kairos moment in our lives. This image, originally created by Mike Breen, illustrates this circle:[1]

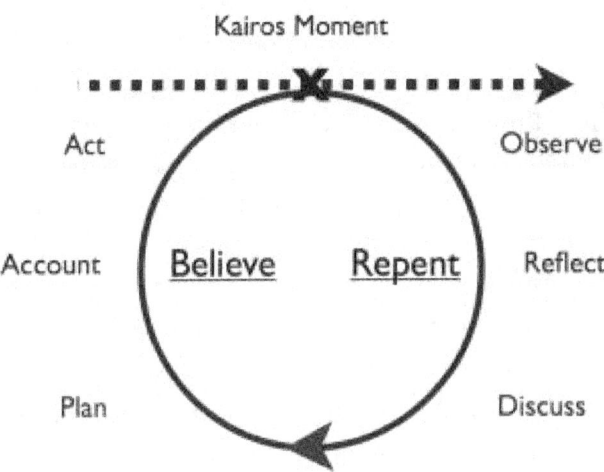

First, we observe. Observing a Kairos moment is the act of recognizing that God is offering us the opportunity to engage more deeply in a moment. This is more difficult than it sounds; we don't often confess our sins to ourselves, much less observe and confess them before God. As we move into reflection, we consider what God may be inviting us to see and respond to.

How might God be moving us toward His heart in inviting us to slow down and reflect on the moment?

The third step may come as a surprise; part of repenting is discussing the opportunity for repentance and change that we are observing and reflecting upon with other Christians who are able to hear our hearts and help us process. This might take place in a weekly time when you connect with others in conversations about faith, like a small group or huddle. Or perhaps you share it with someone in your home or a good friend.

These first three steps constitute the repentance portion of this Learning Circle. While confessing our sins to one another is biblical, and certainly has merit, I also find I can move through this circle with ample observance and reflection, and I don't always need to confess every kairos moment to another person. Sometimes, I find it is enough to hold these moments in the light of God's love and allow Him to speak to me about what is happening in my spiritual life and where I'm being invited to change.

Repenting means turning from something, and that requires turning toward something else! So, in the Kairos Learning Circle, when we repent, we then are moving towards belief. Learning to believe in a new way requires action on our part; we figure out what it looks like to believe God in this specific area of our lives and make a plan to do so. Then we account for the plan, making the needed changes, and act, by living it out.

The thing about kairos moments is that they seem to keep coming around until we respond. It is as though the Spirit invites us to make change, and, when we fail, He invites us once again. God doesn't leave us where we are; He is always inviting us forward. The invitations keep showing up! Part of maintaining good ground, spiritually, is being attuned to the ways the Spirit is moving, and ensuring that we engage each Kairos moment. We open the invitations and respond; this is discipleship.

Good Ground Requires Intentionality and Maintenance

Several years ago, we moved into a home with a more robust landscape; there are lots of different shrubs and flowering plants that preceded our arrival, and maintaining the beds and the yard takes serious effort. We must stay mindful of the season and which plants require pruning, which must be mulched, and where we need to address weeds. We must put down preemergent fertilizer, and sometimes do some seeding work. You get the idea: we can't just let the yard grow and go. The result would be a catastrophe, and we'd lose the hard work and landscape-love of the prior owners.

The same is true in our spiritual lives. Cultivating good ground takes some intentionality and awareness, too. Listening for the Spirit's work, so we can stay in step with the Spirit, requires that our hearts are attuned to the Spirit's presence.

As you practice abiding, or remaining, with Christ, both by drawing away and by yielding to God's active presence in your life moment-by-moment, you will grow in hearing His voice and in your capacity to respond. The more you hear and respond to Jesus, the more you are cultivating the good ground that receives the seed! And that good ground becomes the place for a harvest beyond your wildest dreams, courtesy of our Great God, who never stops sowing.

Be encouraged: by spending time here, you've taken steps
to move in the right direction. Stay attentive for what God
is showing you, and then have the courage to respond in
obedience! Jesus said it this way:

> Steep your life in God-reality, God-initiative,
> God-provisions. Don't worry about missing out.
> You'll find all your everyday human concerns will
> be met. Give your entire attention to what God is
> doing right now, and don't get worked up about
> what may or may not happen tomorrow. God will
> help you deal with whatever hard things come up
> when the time comes. (Matt. 6:33-34)

Listen

Listen—Give this your
attention!
That's what Jesus said.
For ears don't always hear—
sometimes, they're along for
a ride,
and the body can be present
without the mind,

So fixate now on what is
near.
Focus, examine,
Put your mind to this
and see what happens.
Listen.

Listen, really listen!
Lean in to hear
the still small voice
of our Colossal God,
the calculated whisper of
His Gargantuan Presence,
Whose hushed tones
make hearts
halt and pivot.

The right life hinges
on this capacity to
Listen, really listen.

---

1. Mike Breen, Building A Discipling Culture (Sheffield:
3DM Publishing, 2011), 62.

— · —

PRUNING OUR BELOVED BRANCHES

7

You're Blessed When. . . .

Bethel
(based on Gen 28 & 32)

Do you ever find yourself in a
place
where you know it—
where your soul
settles into a certainty,
surely,
God is here.

That's not a declaration,
really
It's more like an admission
of grace upon grace, surely,
God is here.

The whole wide world is all
God's camp, you know
The far-reaching heights,

the deepest depths
There's no where He is not.

So, no matter the landscape
you're standing on today
Yes—whatever terrain
you're traversing, surely,
God is here.

And we, dear friends, are the
wrestlers
suddenly aware
that we urgently require a
blessing,
so we tangle and tussle,
contending for the ending
we desire.
We grapple for grace,
scuffling in perceived
scarcity,
often unaware
that the abundance of Christ
has locked in with us, arm to
arm.
Surely, God is here.

What if we laid down
whatever score
we've been fighting for
to rest in the presence
of the One who loves us

enough
to hold fast, even when we
wrestle?
Especially when we wrestle
because surely, God is here.

We may not strut our stuff on
exit,
rather, we may limp away,
But what if I told you
that hobble
is evidence that the Gospel
has found you, and
you—Him?
Yes, friends,
Surely, God is here.

Recently, I thought I might create a wall of blessing in my home. I've noticed stores are filled with words and phrases I could feature. Here is a sampling from my most recent shopping trip:

- Blessed

- Crazy blessed

- Blessed beyond measure

- Bless this mess

- Simply blessed

- Thankful, Grateful, Blessed

- Bless our nest

- Prayers go up, Blessings come down

Are you getting the vibe of this? The trip left me thinking: *Blessedness sells!* Darn, I think I need this wall in my house! Name it to claim it, right? I mean, if I hang a plaque that names me *crazy blessed*, surely the bestowal of many great things will follow?

(I hope you are reading through these words to hear my sarcasm.)

I've come to believe most of us are not thinking *biblically* when we think about being blessed. And I don't fault us for that: America is permeated with an idea of blessing, and it isn't exactly congruent with Scripture. When Americans talk about blessing, we are generally referring to possessions, upwardly mobile careers, sprawling homes, physical health and well-being, and winning. Generally, lots and lots of winning.

We prefer to see blessing as a commutable condition; something that can be bestowed regardless of one's circumstance (for instance, I could win the lottery tomorrow and be very blessed!). Most often we think this way: the better the circumstances, the better the chance you'd be called "blessed." We don't drive through a neighborhood where people are lacking basics and say, "Wow, this neighborhood is so blessed."

But when Jesus talks about blessing, he speaks very differently. In fact, Jesus ties blessing to experience and place, and it is, quite candidly, the opposite of what we would pick. Consider one of His most famous teaching moments, from his Sermon on the Mount:

You're blessed when you're at the end of your rope. With less of you there is more of God and his rule.

You're blessed when you feel you've lost what is most dear to you. Only then can you be embraced by the One most dear to you.

You're blessed when you're content with just who you are—no more, no less. That's the moment you find yourselves proud owners of everything that can't be bought.

You're blessed when you've worked up a good appetite for God. He's food and drink in the best meal you'll ever eat.

You're blessed when you care. At the moment of being 'care-full,' you find yourselves cared for.

You're blessed when you get your inside world—your mind and heart—put right. Then you can see God in the outside world.

You're blessed when you can show people how

to cooperate instead of compete or fight. That's
when you discover who you really are, and your
place in God's family.

You're blessed when your commitment to God
provokes persecution. The persecution drives you
even deeper into God's kingdom.

Not only that—count yourselves blessed every
time people put you down or throw you out or
speak lies about you to discredit me. What it
means is that the truth is too close for comfort
and they are uncomfortable. You can be glad when
that happens—give a cheer, even!—for though
they don't like it, I do! And all heaven applauds.
And know that you are in good company. My
prophets and witnesses have always gotten into
this kind of trouble. (Matt. 5:3-12)

Do you notice the theme of this passage of Scripture? Every
time Jesus speaks about blessing, he ties it to a *when*—a
condition that, if we are honest, doesn't probably sound like
something we'd choose to focus on. For instance, we'd like to
work up a good appetite for the new trendy eatery, and get
our outside world put right—Facebook polished, Insta-ready.
Most of us spend more time proving we're right than building
consensus. And persecution? Well, we'd rather not experience
that. Who signs up to be at the end of their rope?

It's a bit disorienting, at first read. But perhaps this is
intentional: Jesus is speaking words that are *not* expected.

Most of his listeners would have easily adopted the current American understanding of blessing as prosperity and wealth; we see proof of this in much of the book of Proverbs, for instance, as an example of the cultural understanding of connection between prosperity and blessedness.

It is important to understand, then, that this portion of teaching isn't separating out two kinds of disciples, those who are blessed and those who aren't. Rather, it is pointing toward one kind of condition: the one that makes us aware of our complete dependence on God. And that sort of condition is typically *not* an easy place to be.

On the effortless days of life, we are quite confident to be self-reliant. Things are going well, and we feel a sense of self-determination in all of this well-being, as if we've somehow lived right, causing this smooth outcome. When life is riddled with difficulty, loss, heartache, persecution, or suffering, however, we are immediately aware of how outsized we are by the conditions we face.

Difficult conditions predispose us to seek the Kingdom of God in new and different ways. Blessedness in the Bible isn't about having a perfect life, or all the things, or all the followers, or all the fame! Blessedness in Scripture is about knowing that no matter what you have, *Jesus has you*—and that you are daily drawing closer to Him because of it.

It's not surprising that we tend to reverse the idea of blessing; the Beatitudes that Jesus spoke are, quite frankly, the polar opposite of what our culture espouses as the path to success or blessedness. What the world says, and what the Kingdom promises, are opposed to one another. Jesus turns worldly wisdom upside down. The question, then, is which one will we choose to believe?

Each "when" that Jesus spoke is a statement about complete dependence on God in life. And the result of that utter dependence Is—you guessed it—*blessedness*. But "complete dependence" is not the declarative fodder of most accent walls. Can you imagine hanging a sign that says, "I was discredited today. #blessed!" or "I'm at the end of my rope, feeling so blessed!"

The conditions that Jesus describes here are the ones that will bring us to our knees, crying out with the psalmist, "All of my hope is in You, God."[1]

When Difficulty Meets Jesus

It is interesting to hold these situations that Jesus describes alongside Isaiah 61:1-3, where the ministry of Jesus is foreshadowed. Look at how the places that are named as an aspect of Jesus' ministry speak directly to those places we experience Him most deeply, according to the beatitudes:

> The Spirit of God, the Master, is on me
> because God anointed me.
> He sent me to preach good news to *the poor*,
> heal the heartbroken,
> Announce freedom to all *captives*,
> pardon all *prisoners*.
> God sent me to announce the year of his
> grace—
> a celebration of God's destruction of our

enemies—
and to comfort *all who mourn*,
To care for the needs of all who mourn in Zion,
give them bouquets of roses instead of ashes,
Messages of joy instead of news of doom,
a praising heart instead of a languid spirit.
Rename them "Oaks of Righteousness"
planted by God to display his glory.
(Isa 61:1-3, MSG; italics added)

Jesus has come to speak into these places of heartache and disappointment, of disillusionment and captivity. When we experience seasons that are marked by loss, we also walk in spaces that predispose us to know the nearness of Christ. This is the upside-down work of the Kingdom of God; from our downsized dreams, losses, and broken-heartedness comes the blessing of really knowing Jesus more, as He ushers in healing and hope.

Experiencing the blessedness of the Kingdom of God comes from taking up residence in the person of Jesus. Blessedness in Scripture is as simple as this: active abiding yields a blessed life.

The Necessity of Speaking a Blessing

Theologian Stanley Hauerwas has written, "We can only act within the world we can see, and we can only see the world by being rightly trained to see. We do not come to see just by looking, but by disciplined skills developed through initiation into a narrative."[2] In simpler words, to *act* in the world, we must learn to *see it,* and to *see* Kingdom realities, we must be able to first *say* them. Articulating truth helps us see the truth and then live into it.

The world in which we live doesn't often align with Kingdom-reality, however, so it is vital for us, as Jesus-followers, to speak the truth of how God has said He is at work in the world. If we can see it, then we can finally live it. This is where I think speaking a blessing helps us keep living righteously—or living right with God and with others.

I bless God, people, circumstances, and things on the regular. I don't believe, though, that my blessing brings anything into being that isn't already present. Rather, I believe my blessing rights my own heart and reminds me (and anyone listening) that God is already at work in the situation. How do I know? Because He has said it.

Here are some of the blessings I speak routinely:

- May you be aware of God's presence in the world and join Him in His work.

- May the peace of Christ go before and come behind you, hemming you in.

- May you shine brightly, that others may see the light of Christ in and through you.

- May you know the confidence of Jesus at work in your life today.

- May God use this food to nourish my body, and my body to the glory of His service.

- May I know the strength of Christ at work in me.

- May I lie down and rest in peace, awakening renewed for the next day.

- May I recall that God's mercies are new every morning.

- May I know that God's strength is made perfect in my weakness.

Take note of this important concept; there is no magic here! I am not speaking about anything that isn't already at work. When I bless, I'm acknowledging how God is *already present* and how Jesus is at work in bringing the Kingdom, *right now,* to earth and drawing all people unto Himself. In this way, learning how to speak a blessing rightly orients our hearts and minds to the active presence of Father, Son, and Spirit in our world. Most often, blessedness isn't just now being *bestowed,* rather it is simply just now being *realized.*

I've also found great joy in crafting haikus in this way. Remember the haiku poem from your school years? Haiku is a pattern of verse in counted syllables, five, then seven, then five. Often, I form prayers in haiku:

Expectant Spirit,
Hydrate me with abundance
For my soul is dry.

Great Feast-giving God
Uncertain of my place here
Hand letter my spot.

You say, Do not fear!
But scary is everywhere.
Jesus, be my Peace.

The Times We Wrestle for a Blessing

But, what about Jacob, you may be wondering? Didn't we begin this chapter with the idea, through poetry, that Jacob wrestled God through the night and *demanded* a blessing? Why would this story be included in Scripture, if not to be our model?[3]

These are fair questions, and it should be said that there are times when all that is in us requires a blessing to move forward. I think Jacob was in that space. Having tricked his brother out of a birthright and stolen Esau's firstborn blessing (which was a huge deal!), Jacob fled the scene, and along the way to refuge, he laid his head on a rock and had an important dream. God blessed Jacob, even in the home of Laban, where life wasn't always what we'd call fair.

When Jacob gets the word to go back to his land, he will have to face his past. His choices have caught up with him! Jacob is afraid, and on the journey back home with all of his people, there comes a night where Jacob finds himself completely alone—except, of course, he isn't.

We are never alone. I hope you know that!

God is on the scene, in the form of an angel—a co-wrestler—and an all-night wrestling match ensues. Scripture tells us that Jacob refuses to let go until he receives a blessing.

There are times in life, certainly, when we struggle to speak the blessing that is already at work. In those moments, like Jacob, our struggle to seek a blessing turns into a more physical endeavor, a demanding of the heart and soul to know that God is, indeed, present and that He will lock arms with us when we need Him most.

Is it possible that this story exists in the pages of Scripture so we can know, without a shout of a doubt, that when we find ourselves in the darkest night and begin to think we are all alone, God Himself will arm-wrestle with us, and we can even boldly demand the blessing that we desperately need?

Jacob emerges from the wrestling match with two things changed: he is the recipient of a new name, and he now limps. Each of these is significant in different ways, although they may be lost on the modern reader.

The new name, *Israel,* is a change in identity at the core. In Jacob's day, a given name conveyed a promise. It was what you would become. So Jacob, whose name means "heel," marked his position in life, grasping at the heel of his brother Esau. It could also be translated as deceiver, or trickster. What a word for parents to speak over a child, right? Maybe it is no wonder that Jacob struggled and needed to wrestle through this struggle of identity.

But Jacob is also God's child, and God will now name him Israel. Israel means *wrestled with God*, or *God struggles*, or even *God rules*. Whoa.

Named from his experience, Israel carries forth the truth that God will, in fact, lock arms with us at our lowest point, and stay with us until we emerge, changed. But, friends, we will limp.

Israel is marked by the moment when he encountered God, and physically, he now has a daily reminder of this divine interaction. How might God be marking you in this season of wrestling? If you are struggling to speak out the blessing that is unfolding in your life, hang on tight—because God is surely here.

Living the Questions

For most of us, answers have
become like oxygen;
We need them to live.
Tidy little certainties to all
the ponderings:
Which way should I go?
Is this person the one?
How will I know?

Should I take a new job?
Why did this happen?
Why didn't that happen?
What will happen next?
What if it doesn't?
And we gasp for answers like
we're
suffocating in a room
without air.

The more we depend on
answers,
the more dependent we
become on answers.
What if, instead, we
embraced uncertainty
as one way God leads us
toward greater trust?
What if we lived the
questions,
and allowed faith the space
to show us
how to keep breathing
through ambiguity and
pain?
Instead of living for answers,
let's live for Jesus—and
remember that He asked
more questions than
anything.

> Let's live the questions,
> starting now.

---

1. Psalm 38:15; Psalm 39:7; Psalm 56: 3-4; Psalm 62:1, 5-6, 8

2. Stanley Hauerwas, "The Demands of a Truthful Story: Ethics and the Pastoral Task," Chicago Studies 21 (1982): 65–66.

3. The story of Jacob wrestling with God occurs in Genesis 32; in order to understand the broader narrative, however, consider reading Genesis 24–33.

8

— • —

PRAYING THROUGH

On Prayer

God is like stars in the city
sky:
always present, not always
visible to the human eye.
Like the chirp, chirp
when one pours out their
soul in prayer
and hears crickets.

Is God speaking through
that
chirp, chirp?
Should we discern
something profound
in the relative silence
between?

Perhaps, the cricket's

stridulation
is an invitation
to lean in with intention
and listen for words not
audibly spoken
but indelibly pressed upon a
soul.

Chirp, chirp.
Resounding without
sounding.
And yes, there's no doubt
stars cascade the city sky,
too.
Revealed yet concealed.

This is faith. Lean in.

Several months into a difficult season, I was listening to
the online stream of a friend preaching. My friend, Vernon
Gordon, was laying out some serious truth, and I was agreeing
with him all along the way. Then he said something like this,
"Many of us need to start speaking *to* the struggle. We're
good at speaking *about* the struggle. We tell our friends, our
coworkers, our family, all about our struggle. But we need to
be speaking *to* the struggle."

Immediately, I knew deep down that he was right. I'd been complaining, a lot, to anyone who would listen about how hard this time was in my life. I'd spent hours talking *about* my struggle. But speaking *to* it? No, I hadn't done much of that.

Something awakened in me that morning, and I want to offer it to you now: when you are in a season where you feel you are losing ground, prayer is the number one way you change your position. This is because prayer is a way of speaking to *Jesus* about our struggles, and also gives us the opportunity to speak *to* the struggle, in Jesus's name.

When life is complicated and days are long, knowing what and how to pray seems to be more difficult, as well. Maybe you're wondering: If God already knows every hair on my head, surely he also knows about this hardship I'm facing; why do I also need to pray about it? This is a fair question. What does an active prayer life accomplish in us?

Perhaps you've bought in on the importance of prayer, but you wonder whether you're doing it right. Is it okay to pray a certain way about this situation? How, exactly, should I pray about this?

We're going to seek out some answers to these questions in this chapter. I have a loftier goal, though, and I'll state it plainly here for you: I want you to finish this chapter feeling reenergized about prayer and your capacity to not only pray for your situation, but to pray *through* your situation. But before we talk more about prayer, we've got to go all the way back to where this section began, with a key verse from the book of James:

"Consider it a sheer gift, friends, when tests and
challenges come at you from all sides. You know
that under pressure, your faith-life is forced into
the open and shows its true colors. So don't try
to get out of anything prematurely. Let it do its
work so you become mature and well-developed,
not deficient in any way." (James 1:2-4)

Now, let's look at the same verse a the widely used translation,
the NRSV:

"My brothers and sisters, whenever you face trials
of any kind, consider it nothing but joy, because
you know that the testing of your faith produces
endurance; and let endurance have its full effect,
so that you may be mature and complete, lacking
in nothing." (James 1:2-4, NRSV)

In both translations, we see the idea of a progression in our
faith life that comes from facing challenges or trials: faith
brings about endurance, and endurance helps us to become
mature and complete. It's essential that we recognize this end
goal, because in the midst of hardship, when we are not quite
sure what is being produced as a result of all of this, we can
return to this section of Scripture to remind our hearts that,
indeed, there is a purpose or goal in all of this, and it is to bring
about something good in us. It is to bring about completeness
and maturity in our spiritual lives; this is how hardship and

trial are used in the life of the believer. But to attain the goal, we must first endure, or persevere, through the trial.

Perseverance is a funny word; we think we understand it, but until we've truly lived a season of perseverance, it's hard to put our arms around what this word means. Another way of thinking about perseverance is a passionate patience.[1] Patience is a necessary component because we recognize an end goal that is far beyond this trial or hardship, and we are patiently working toward it as we persevere. The idea of passion comes from the internal desire for that goal to be achieved. We can persevere through very difficult things, when we understand the goal or end that we are working toward, and desire that outcome with our whole heart.

Setbacks, hardship, and suffering are, to our spiritual life, as weight training is to the physical body. The more we endure in healthy ways, the stronger we become. Some of the most inspirational people in the world have overcome great odds to be in these places; some of our greatest spiritual leaders have endured much hardship in order to bring the depth of wisdom and insight that qualifies their leadership as exceptional.

One way of developing spiritual perseverance is through prayer. This means that prayer does as much for us, in our spiritual lives, as it does in our relationship with God. The right practice of prayer helps us to persevere through the most difficult times.

Prayer Brings About Godly Perspective

Remembering that as humans, we are prone to self-reliance, a primary way that we lean into God-reliance is through the posture of prayer. Bringing ourselves to God in prayer puts several things on display. First, it shows our need for Him—for His presence, grace, and help in our time of need. Second, it shows our belief that God is listening, cares about us, and shows up on our behalf. So prayer is both an expression of need and a display of faith. Even when we aren't sure what to pray, showing up to admit this to God is a critical posture for our spiritual self.

Prayer is a way of counting God in. Many times in life, we are tempted to count God out, assuming that He doesn't care or has more important things to do. Sometimes we convince ourselves that God won't act on our behalf or is far removed from our circumstance. These are ways of counting God out. However, Scripture is clear—when we see a gap between what we experience of God and what we know is possible, we are to be bold and persistent in prayer.

Multiple stories prove this out in the pages of Scripture. For instance, in Luke 11, Jesus tells a story about someone who needs to borrow bread from a neighbor for an unexpected house guest. It's late at night; they knock at the neighbor's door and explain the situation. But the neighbor says that it's late—the kids are in bed—and they aren't getting up to help. Jesus asserts that the neighbor will eventually get up and provide the needed bread, if the one knocking doesn't give up, because the one knocking will start waking the others in the area, too. It's a funny visual for what it looks like to pray and not give up!

In another story Jesus tells about prayer in Luke 18, there is a judge who doesn't care about justice for a widow that is being treated poorly. The widow keeps showing up to ask for help. Eventually, the judge is motivated to help, not because he starts caring more about justice or even what the people of the town may think, but simply because he is being continually bothered by the persistence of the mistreated widow.

These stories can be a bit confusing to the reader. You may wonder, for instance: Is God supposed to be like the neighbor who is sleeping and doesn't want to be bothered? Or is God like the unjust judge, who doesn't care about setting things right in the world? I can see how a reader may ask this question. However, thankfully, neither could be further from the truth!

Remember the concept of agency? These parables aren't about God's action, or agency, in the matter at hand, but rather about ours. We are to be like the one who needs bread and doesn't stop knocking. We are to be like the widow who knows there is someone who can make things right for her, and so she keeps coming back for justice.

It was common in Jesus's day for rabbis to use a lesser-to-greater argument in proving a point. Consider the lilies of the field; how much more will God clothe you? Consider the sparrow; how much more does God know your need?

Consider the neighbor who needs bread for a guest; how much more should you keep knocking when you have a real need in your life? Consider the widow who is being mistreated; how much more should you pursue justice, for yourself and for others, through prayer?

Be bold! Persist! When there is a gap between what you see in circumstance and what you believe could be possible, don't shy away from asking God to move. Instead, lean in and don't stop asking until you see what you need. Jesus encourages us through these stories to pray and not give up.

Developing Perseverance is Crucial to Faith

More than just a good skill to put on a spiritual resume, perseverance is one of the most crucial skills in the life of faith. The end goal of spiritual life is to be formed in the image of Jesus; to bring Him glory and honor. This allows our lives to point others toward the Lifegiver. Sometimes we confuse the end goal of character with our desired outcome as humans of a life of comfort! Jesus never calls anyone in the pages of the Bible to a life of comfort. He does, however, call disciples to lay down their lives and find themselves in Him.

For most modern-day disciples, the idea of true surrender is foreign, and it may even feel far-fetched, like it is something for the super-saints. How does that Christlike character get formed in a Christ follower? How does the average, everyday disciple grow to be more like Christ?

The answer, according to Scripture, is in the very trials, setbacks, and suffering that we face and so often want to avoid. Consider this passage from Romans 5:

> There's more to come: We continue to shout
> our praise even when we're hemmed in with
> troubles, because we know how troubles can
> develop passionate patience in us, and how
> that patience in turn forges the tempered steel
> of virtue, keeping us alert for whatever God

will do next. In alert expectancy such as this,
we're never left feeling shortchanged. Quite the
contrary—we can't round up enough containers
to hold everything God generously pours into our
lives through the Holy Spirit! (Rom. 5:3-5)

What can troubles develop in us, according to this passage?
Yes—passionate patience. That is the very perseverance we've
been talking about! And this ability to persevere? It leads to
"the tempered steel of virtue," which other translations call
"character." *Dokime*, the Greek word that is being translated
here as character, or as the tempered steel of virtue, is
only found six times in the whole of Scripture. *Dokime* is
a proving-out of character, and it can also be translated
"approved, tried character."[2]

To be completely clear, *dokime* is not about just building
good character through trials. We're talking about building
godly character through those troubles and setbacks. Godly
character is worth it. Learning more of the nature and
temperament of Jesus through the difficulty and suffering we
face, as we persevere in prayer over these moments where we
feel we're losing ground, produces the sheer gift of passionate
patience. Passionate patience tempers us and creates godly
character.

Tempering is a process of strengthening steel or other
alloys that involves heating up the alloy and letting it cool,
repeatedly. The more this happens, the stronger the substance
becomes. But that's not all that is being accomplished in the
repetitive heating and cooling: the more steel or any other
alloy experiences the rapid temperature change from hot to

cold, the more flexible it becomes as well. To be strong and flexible, we must also endure the heating and cooling of trials. Tempering increases the toughness by decreasing the hardness of the ferrous alloy. Considering this metaphor for the spiritual character we are trying to achieve, what a great outcome this would be for us, to help us be formed in the image of Christ! Prayer helps us to stay in the fire and keep hope about what is being produced in us in the midst of it.

Hope Follows Tempering

The ultimate outcome of trials and tests is a deeper hope in the person of Christ. Romans 5 tells us that character leads to this hope. Hope is another word that benefits from a definition. Biblically, hope is not about wishing—it isn't a desire for something we dream could be. It's not the Disney version of wishing upon a star. Hope, rather, is what we've come to know can be. It is, as Peterson aptly describes it, "alert expectancy."

When we hope, we are alert, because we are looking out for what is coming. Expectancy follows, because we are believing what we know to be true of who God is. Hebrews 6:19 tells us that this sort of hope is an anchor, or (as Peterson translates it) an "unbreakable spiritual lifeline." Dropping this anchor, holding fast to this lifeline, is the work of prayer.

Prayer is an Active Verb

When we think about prayer, it is easy to frame it as something we *do* to try to bring about something we *hope for*—as though it is an action that *causes* an outcome. While this can be true, prayer is not only about bringing about a desired outcome in our spiritual lives.

Prayer is also, of itself, an outcome. It is an expression of passionate patience before the Father. Prayer is a way of practicing alert expectancy. Prayer, in and of itself, is an active event.

Esther Fleece Allen writes that the Hebrew words for "remember" and "not forget" (*zakar* and *lo shakach*) are grammatically active. "These are 'doing' verbs! Remembering is not a passive reflection, but a bold action of calling God's truth into the present. This practice is found in both the Old and New Testaments."[3]

Indeed, the act of prayer is far more than a passive reflection. We aren't simply holding concerns before God when we pray. Rather, we are actively reminding ourselves of who God is and how He is at work in the world, and in our lives. Prayer is an active-voice and present-tense pursuit.

We don't engage in this sort of reminding prayer when we simply bring a list of concerns and roll through them almost as if by rote. That sort of lowest-common-denominator prayer is a far distance from the way Jesus paints the prayer life.

Imagine, for a moment, the widow crying out for justice. Remember the neighbor who has nothing to offer their guest and beats on the door of another in the middle of the night until the door is answered and the need is met. There is nothing list-like about this sort of prayer; it is fervent and expectant. How do we learn to pray this way?

Using Scripture as a Guide

We often wonder what to pray for, or how to pray about a situation or circumstance. The good news is that God's Word is full of inspiration and ideas about how and what to pray. For instance, consider using the psalms as a starting point for honest prayer. Try locating a psalm that expresses the desire of your heart, and then substituting your own name in the flow of the verses, or the name of someone you are praying for. This is a powerful way to put new words to the things on our hearts as we come to pray.

Scripture holds many promises for us, as believers, and these promises can be spoken over situations and circumstances as a way of reminding ourselves and reminding God of what He has said. For instance, Romans 8:28 is a portion of Scripture that holds a promise that most of us are familiar with. Consider it here, in the Message translation:

> Meanwhile, the moment we get tired in the waiting, God's Spirit is right alongside helping us along. If we don't know how or what to pray, it doesn't matter. He does our praying in and for us, making prayer out of our wordless sighs, our aching groans. He knows us far better than we know ourselves, knows our pregnant condition, and keeps us present before God. That's why we can be so sure that every detail in our lives of love for God is worked into something good. (Rom. 8:28)

To pray this over a situation, here's how I might use these words and ideas:

Lord, I confess that I'm tired of waiting. That moment is here—Your word says that Your Spirit is also here to help me. I don't know what to pray for. I wish I knew the right words. But You are praying for me, even as my heart breaks. You know me far better than I know myself, and you know all the things I'm carrying. You know what is coming, too—all the things You are preparing to bring about in my life. I'm counting on You, God, for every detail! I'm counting on You to work all of this for good, because this is what You've promised. I don't see how this will happen, but I am believing it can happen, and it will happen—because You've said that this is so, and You always keep Your Word. Help my heart to believe, too.

Some of the most powerful prayers we can ever pray come directly out of Scripture. The Bible helps us to remember to pray boldly, and with real words, expectant for what God can and will do on our behalf.

What to Pray in Difficult Times

Finding the right words to offer to God when life is difficult can feel a bit challenging. In Philippians, we read these words:

> Don't fret or worry. Instead of worrying, pray.
> Let petitions and praises shape your worries
> into prayers, letting God know your concerns.
> Before you know it, a sense of God's wholeness,
> everything coming together for good, will come
> and settle you down. It's wonderful what happens
> when Christ displaces worry at the center of your
> life. (Phil. 4:6-7)

The idea of letting petitions and praises shape our worries into prayers is helpful to me. In the Greek, the idea of making known, declaring, or discovering is in this text, and it is a present, continuous, repeated sort of this making known, declaring, and discovering activity.

With this in mind, it is appropriate in prayer to tell God just what we need. If you aren't sure about what you need, start by confessing that. We can pray directly for what we desire in a circumstance, with boldness, and we can keep offering that up to the Lord. Alongside that, we hold space for how God is moving, and ask Him to help our hearts with whatever the outcome might be.

When we pray, it is good to state the obvious! Jesus routinely invites people to state their need, even when it is evident. Take a look at His miracles, and note how they are often preceded by words like, "What do you want me to do for you?" and "Do you want me to come and heal him?" Stating the obvious is a part of honest communication with God, and it is for us—not for Him. Asking for what we need builds faith and confidence in our great God, who can accomplish more than we can ask or even imagine!

Don't underestimate the importance of the idea of discovery. With the Holy Spirit as our guide, when we hold concerns and circumstances in the light of God's love, we discover more deeply who God is, and what we need in this situation. This is why listening is crucial in prayer life, and it is another reason why I recommend a journal.

Praying Through

Part of the challenge of faith is learning to navigate the tensions of what we believe to be true and what we see in our circumstances. That's actually the way the Bible speaks about what faith is, in a passage that helps us think about what it means to trust God and live an extraordinary life marked by His presence. Consider these words:

> The fundamental fact of existence is that this trust in God, this faith, is the firm foundation under everything that makes life worth living. It's our handle on what we can't see. The act of faith is what distinguished our ancestors, set them above the crowd. (Heb. 11:1-2)

These are the words I cannot get away from: "It's our handle on what we can't see."

In a volatile, unstable, complex and ambiguous world, there are so many things we simply can't see. There are things we thought we knew that are all somehow different now; disappointment and heartache that is tough to name, much less move through. There is a very real loss for us all, individually and collectively.

The landscape is just different enough to be disorienting. We desperately need a handle on what we cannot see. This is where faith comes in.

The remainder of the eleventh chapter in Hebrews is a roll call of sorts for the giants of faith. We hear about people like Noah, Abraham, Sarah, and Enoch. (Remember Enoch? He's the one who skipped right over death and went straight to be with God!) We know the whole stories of each of these faith giants; we see their stories in light of what happened during their lives—and also how their stories continued long afterward. We see the result of their incredible faith.

Many of them didn't ever see the full result of their incredible faith. About half of those listed in this passage didn't live to see the complete fruit of their obedience, or the way that what they hoped for ultimately came to be, in part because of their faith and faithfulness. Perhaps if we were to sit with some of these faith giants in their last days, they would tell us that faith was the handle on what they could not see.

It's also like that for us. We're in the midst of a far greater story than our small lives will tell. Faith requires that we passionately persevere in the midst of hardship, and that we continue to circle our concerns boldly in prayer before God, remembering that He longs to redeem and restore, and that He is actively setting all things right, even now. Yes, *especially* now.

Amen

Amen!
So be it!
God, bring it!
Let it happen,
make it so.

From weary lips
words rise
to the ears of our
Inexhaustible God
Who never stops listening
and acting.
Expect it.
When you pray,
Look for God's powerful
hand.
So, Yes—and Amen!
So be it!
God, bring it!
All of our hope
rests in You.

1. This word choice is found in Peterson's translation, The Message.
2. https://www.biblestudytools.com/lexicons/greek/nas/dok ime.html.
3. https://www.faithgateway.com/reminding-god-to-reme mber/#.YijESejMLIV.

9

—·—

RESETTING YOUR PASSWORDS

Bless the Lord

Bless the Lord,
O my soul,
let all that is within me
bless His holy name.

Rest in the Lord,
O my soul,
let me cease striving and
learn
to rest in His holy name.

Peace in the Lord,
O my soul,
let my innermost self find
that
Abiding Peace is His holy
name.

Trust, hope, and wait on the
Lord,
O my soul!
Let me always live
expectantly and
bless His holy name.

It was mid-summer, the time of year where people are laughing by the pool, celebrating June's bounty of fruits, and relaxing in the long-lit days of sunshine. But I had just journaled about how I was dwindling to nothingness. So focused was I on the ground I was losing, that I could hardly see the flowers unfurling and hear the bees buzzing by, busily pollinating. I was only looking down.

Have you been in one of those seasons? Maybe you are there now. When it seems we are losing ground, we do tend to look down, don't we? We survey the loss and ruminate on what seems to be taken away. My focus was so homed in on the loss about me, the loss of identity and the lack of direction, that I began to see less and less of how God was at work both in and around me.

But we agreed on a truth early on in this book, so I'm bringing it back around now: anywhere you've got footprints, you can confidently look for God's fingerprints. This is true, even if you don't feel it, or see those fingerprints around you.

I know this to be true for several reasons. First, Scripture tells us that God hems us in, before and behind.[1] That means we go nowhere apart from Him.

We're also told that we can't go anywhere apart from His presence! That's a major theme of Psalm 139:

> Is there anyplace I can go to avoid your Spirit?
> to be out of your sight?
> If I climb to the sky, you're there!
> If I go underground, you're there!
> If I flew on morning's wings
> to the far western horizon,
> You'd find me in a minute—
> you're already there waiting!
> Then I said to myself, 'Oh, he even sees me in the dark!
> At night I'm immersed in the light!'
> It's a fact: darkness isn't dark to you;
> night and day, darkness and light, they're all the same to you.
> (Ps 139:7-12)

Anywhere we are, God is there. It's just easier to *forget* this truth when you feel you're losing at life, or you're being downsized or diminished in some area, or you are struggling with hard ground.

We say to ourselves, *is God with me?* And we answer: *of course He is!* But the eighteen inches from our head to our heart feels long when we are challenged in life; sometimes when we know the truth in our minds, our hearts are struggling to keep pace.

And that's where I was in mid-June.

Why Focus is Key in Spiritual Life

It's a funny thing about focus: what we focus on always grows. For instance, have you ever car-shopped and begun to narrow your search to a certain make or model, or even a color of vehicle? All of a sudden, you will see those vehicles everywhere! You may have thought them to be rare before, but now, they are parked at the grocery store, someone on your street may even drive this model of car, and when you are on the interstate, you see them on your right and left.

Why does this happen? It's simple really: you've begun to focus on this make or model of car. The vehicles were always there, but you just weren't focused on them, so you didn't notice them amid your daily life and routine.

The same is true in our spiritual lives. When our eyes are focused on what we're losing in life, whether that be some part of our identity, a job, a medical situation, a relationship, something financial, or even the life of someone we love, the sense of lost ground will only grow. We will see it in all parts of our life; it will overtake our days and mark our mornings and evenings. I know, because I've been there.

But then, on that morning in mid-June, the Holy Spirit broke in with some truth.

The Call to Reset

I was reading the Bible that morning, and I came upon Psalm 89. The psalm was my last part of the reading for the day, and I was cruising along in the Message translation until I came to verses 15-18, which were like a blinking red light signaling for me to stop in the midst of my otherwise steady-green-light morning reading:

> Blessed are the people who know the passwords of
> praise,
> who shout on parade in the bright presence of
> God.
> Delighted, they dance all day long; they know
> who you are, what you do—they can't keep it
> quiet!
> Your vibrant beauty has gotten inside us—
> you've been so good to us! We're walking on air!
> All we are and have we owe to God,
> Holy God of Israel, our King! (Ps 89:15-18)

I thought, wait, what? The passwords of praise? There is such a thing as passwords of praise? And then the Holy Spirit whispered to my heart: You need a password reset, Christy.

When Passwords Are Complicated

I've struggled as of late with passwords. They are getting so complex! Just when I think I've got a few in rotation, the requirements change. Add capitals, but also include lowercase letters. Use symbols. Your password must include a number!

My brain can only hold so much data. So I got this little pink book to try to manually capture the multitude of changing passwords that our house must know at any given moment in order to stay connected and thrive.

I have about a 50-percent success rate of putting the passwords into the book. This is deeply problematic when I happen upon a site that requires a password I haven't recorded. The guessing game begins, and it is never pretty. Sometimes I am a great guesser, and sometimes I get the dreaded lockout.

Peterson's translation, the "passwords of praise," introduces a question for me: Can we be locked out, spiritually? While Scripture is clear that nothing can separate us from the love of God, forgetting the passwords of praise does bring about a disconnect. When we leave behind thanksgiving in a hard season, this omission reduces our capacity to see God at work.

That's because praise and thanksgiving have a specific function in our lives. Not only do they honor God, but they also help us actively place our trust in God and rehearse who He is, regardless of what we see.

So the psalmist proclaimed that we're blessed when we remember these passwords! Remember, blessedness isn't about having a perfect life, or all the things, or all the followers, or all the fame! Blessedness in Scripture is about knowing that no matter what you have or don't have in this life, Jesus has you—and you are daily drawing closer to Him because of it.

Knowing the passwords of praise helps us to be aware of the closeness of Christ in any circumstance, whether life feels smooth and all downhill, or it's the most difficult, uphill path you've ever walked. When the road is straightforward, it is far simpler to acknowledge God's presence with us. That's just how life works. Easy days, uncomplicated praise.

But what about when the journey is on a steep path, the kind of path where we feel like the places to put our feet are more narrow and the obvious, accessible ground is disappearing? What, then, can we offer thanks for?

Further Defining the Passwords of Praise

Trying to better understand how Peterson landed on the phrase "passwords of praise" as his translation choice here, I journeyed back into the original Hebrew to better understand the text. The word in this passage translates more literally as the "festal shout," and it also includes the concepts of acclaiming joy or the battle cry. Suddenly, I understood exactly why Peterson chose the phrase "passwords of praise."

Have any of us experienced the festal shout? Can we wrap our minds around experience with a battle cry? More often than not, we answer both with a resounding no. We need a more accessible language to understand these concepts.

So what was the festal shout about? This was a communal and collective expression of the joy of being in God's steadfast love. It was a shout about His faithfulness, and it happened when a group was gathered together. We're talking about a very loud shout here; something akin to the crowd going wild at an outdoor concert when an artist starts their signature song, the one that everyone gathered has been waiting for. I hope you're getting an idea of the sort of communal cry this festal shout might be!

It was also a common practice at the time this psalm was written for an army to lead off in battle with a loud, resounding cry. (I'm picturing Mel Gibson in *Braveheart*, letting out a massive war cry.) It's significant, then, that this passage evokes the idea of a battle cry; we don't want to forget that shout when we're moving into uncertain territory. The battle cry is a rallying call for the troops; it moves them forward in unity. All of these ideas are encompassed in the word choice of the psalmist.

Here's a funny thing: my laptop doesn't even recognize the word festal. It flags it every time I key it in! This is not a concept we're familiar with, but we know all about passwords in this day and age. We've experienced the forgetting, the guessing game that follows, and even the dreaded lockout. It's all part of the world in which we are living, so Peterson translates the psalm with words that tap into our understanding: Blessed are the people who know the passwords of praise!

Since we've just spent an entire chapter on the biblical idea of blessing, it isn't surprising that this beatitude of sorts positions blessing alongside being able to remember why we praise, even amid difficulty. Scripture tells us that God inhabits the praises of His people, so we know that any time we are speaking His praises, He is present in this moment in a very intimate way. Again, abiding in Christ brings blessedness. But what, exactly, are the passwords we should be speaking?

The Unchanging Character of Jesus

When the ground beneath us has shifted and life has changed quickly, it is helpful to remember these words, "For Jesus doesn't change—yesterday, today, tomorrow, he's always totally himself" (Heb 13:8). No matter how much life around us changes, the One who is with us doesn't shift—ever.

There is no part of who Jesus is that may change today, or tomorrow. So what we know to be true of Jesus, we can continue to count on. People disappoint us, jobs change, our finances diminish, careers are downsized, and relationships end. Through it all, Jesus is rock steady. No matter what is happening around us, or what has happened to us, Jesus can be counted on. He doesn't change. His love endures. He is faithful.

In times when we feel disappointed by life, it is essential to separate the things that have happened from who we know Jesus to be. One way we do this is by rehearsing what God has revealed about His character to us in Scripture.

The psalms are an excellent place to go to understand more of who God is, because people are praising Him in these passages, which were really songs of praise, for who they have known Him to be. Along with the psalmists, we can acclaim these truths about God: He is a Mighty Fortress, our Strong Tower (Ps 18:2), a very present help in time of need or trouble (Ps 46:1). Putting our focus on the character of God in our lives once again helps us to right-size the gospel; what we focus on, grows. Circumstances will discourage us; God's character will always and only encourage us.

Look Back to Look Forward

In uncertain times, it can be tremendously helpful to look back at God's faithfulness in order to move forward. What has His track record been in your life? Take a day to journal some of the times you've seen God work that are "only God" places. If you've been following Jesus, I know that you have these places in your life. Naming them helps to buoy our faith and helps our hearts to hope again.

Consider the names of God and Jesus, as revealed in Scripture. Where have you most come to know the Lord in your life, and what name do you most need to experience now? Naming who God is and how He is showing up in our lives is a part of acclaiming His goodness and mentally capturing His faithfulness.

Establishing Spiritual Permanence

Young children go through a phase where they don't yet understand object permanence. During this time, mom or dad is present and then steps away, and the child is inconsolable: they don't yet understand that their parents will return.

This same concept applies to spiritual life. As we rehearse the promises, character, and provision of God in our lives, and as we focus on the faithfulness of Jesus and how we've known His love, we are working to establish spiritual permanence.[2] The further we walk with Jesus and the more we know and experience His goodness, the more opportunity we have to rehearse His presence. As we do this, our sense of that presence as an unshakable and permanent force in our lives grows. This is spiritual permanence, and it is being built as you walk through trials and difficult seasons choosing to remember and trust the person and character of Christ.

Reclaim the Nearness of Christ

In seasons where we struggle to find God at work, we sometimes need to reclaim His presence. It's important to understand, this doesn't change His proximity to us—not at all! Rather, it changes our awareness of His proximity to us.

One way to increase awareness of God's presence is through an Ignation practice that involves a candle. The candle is used to physically represent the presence of Christ, and the steps are simple. When you are aware of the presence of Christ, you light the candle. Also, when you are in desperate need to be aware of the presence of Christ, you light the candle. It serves as a visual reminder that His presence is near at all times: when we confidently see how God is at work, He is with us, and when we struggle to name how He is at work but feel desperate to see Him moving, He is also—equally—with us.

Some years ago, I stopped praying for the presence of Christ, and began praying for awareness of His presence. I would encourage you to pray the same: *Lord, I know you are close; help me to see and know your nearness in new and intimate ways.*

We can count on God to answer this prayer. His presence is always with us, because Christ lives within us. Sometimes we must simply reclaim that truth for our hearts and minds to know it once more.

Choose Trust

When we remember the passwords of praise, we are actively placing our trust in Christ. Rehearsing who God is, regardless of what we see, is a way of voicing trust in Him. Another way of practicing the choice of trust is, once again, through index cards. In my stack of index cards, there is one that simply reads:

I CHOOSE TRUST. On days when I most need those words, I carry the card around with me and rehearse this choice.

In fact, some days, if you were a fly on the wall, you'd hear the occasional, "I don't see you today, Lord, but I know you are here!" "I'm choosing to trust You right now, God, because You are faithful and You have never let me down." "I know you are doing a new thing in me, Jesus, because your resurrection power is at work in me. I can't perceive it—but I trust You! Yes, I trust You!"

I'm also very mindful about the music I choose as the soundtrack for my day. Songs that revisit God's faithfulness, or put music to His promises, are especially comforting and grounding in uncertain times. Think hard about your inputs in life, when you are trying to remember the passwords of praise: if you are struggling to voice the goodness of God, surround yourself with those who are already there, and see what happens in your own heart and mind. I believe you will find yourself in a space of gratitude and thanksgiving, as your heart remembers who God is and His faithfulness to you.

As you bask in the love of Jesus, He will minister to you in profound ways, and the passwords of praise will return to your mind, your lips, and most importantly, your soul. May you overflow with gratitude for the great and loving God who is unchanging, who never fails, and who surrounds you moment to moment with His presence and peace.

Thanksgiving

Gratitude is about receiving,
with thanks:
It is both rejoicing in
answered prayer,
and rehearsing that God is
able
to do exceedingly
abundantly
more than we can ask or
imagine.

Thanksgiving is
celebrating what God has
done,
holding space for what is,
and believing that God
works
all things for good.

Today is
hands-full-of-blessings
alongside
hands-open-and-expectant-
to-receive.
Gratitude overflows in every
circumstance
because our God is faithful.

Give thanks today, and every
day.

---

1. Psalm 139:5
2. Cloud, Changes that Heal, 64.

WAITING FOR NEW GROWTH

10

— · —

THE FALLOW FIELD

The God of Strange Math

Lately, life has felt like a
zero-sum game
where I'm the biggest loser.
Do you ever have those days?
I treat zero like a digit
unappreciated, filled with
doubt:
Add it, I'm nowhere further
Multiplied, it takes values
out.

But You are the God of
Strange Math,
for when you inhabit the
center
Zeros can bring abundance
Making other numbers
better.

I can see You at the white
board
working with my circled
frame,
But I cannot guess the
outcome
Your equations will arrange.
Though I struggle with my
value
when I yield it to Your hands
Your Expo marks up
miracles
I'll never understand.

Yes, You are the God of
Strange Math,
so remind this heart today
that my zero can be made
hero
holding space for greater
things.

I crave productivity like I crave good, dark chocolate.

If you look closely, you might also find some of my checkboxes
are quite trivial. I give myself credit for everything. Workout?
Check! Shower? Check! Ridiculous? Maybe. But, if you're
wired at all like me, when the box-checking cadence slows for

any reason and productivity seems to drop in your life, the results are disorienting.

So many of us experienced this in some form or fashion during the pandemic, and for many of us, the decreased productivity continues. A friend, whom I consider to be highly productive, mentioned recently that she is currently running at about 40 percent of her regular productivity. I found myself nodding along, knowing that feeling. It's not a feeling I've welcomed, but I'm learning to make peace with churning out less, or even nothing, because I've come to believe that times where I'm not producing externally are often wildly productive, internally. I didn't come to this idea quickly, but the longer I've operated in a space of more margin and less output, the more I've seen a deep-seated peace return to my life, accompanied by new levels of depth in my spiritual life and relationship with God.

But before we delve into what's happening *internally* when we've not got a lot to show for ourselves *externally*, we need to talk about how hard it is to be in a season of limited output. To understand why this is difficult, it's necessary to understand how we're wired.

Set Points and Production-as-worth Mentality

Psychologists theorize that each of us has a "set point"—a preferred level of functioning in life. I confess that my set point is pretty high: my preferred level of output is on the production-heavy end. I'm the person who writes down the thing I just did, so I can check it off the list.

Not everyone is wired to desire so many outputs, but rare is the individual who feels fine resting and never being able to point to something productive in a day. If you're that person, you can probably skip this chapter! But for most of us, when human beings aren't also "doing," anxiety seems to set in.

The unspoken rule is the busier you are, the more worthy you are. If someone is truly important, it follows, we think that their calendar is over-full. To make matters more complicated, social media skews to a heavy output orientation: *Look at what I did!* and *See what my kids accomplished?* and *Check out my latest. . . .*

The fruit of productivity seems to be always on display. There's nothing wrong with celebrating life, of course! But, in a season of decreased output, this form of show-and-tell can feel both heavy and pointless: heavy, because you can't keep up, and pointless, because you feel you've got nothing to show or say. I know this because I've been there, too. There are periods of time where I've watched others contribute to social channels without actually posting myself, uncertain of what to say or how to even show up. If you're there now, you're not alone—and this chapter is especially important for you.

The Internal Drive to Produce

The root of our desire to perform or produce is often an underlying insecurity: our identity and sense of worth are wrapped up in outcomes. We've bought the narrative that output validates our worth. We're busy earning our place in this society, showing others that we've got what it takes and, yes, we are important.

Of course, this is not what Jesus tells us! In Christ, we are more than enough, and that is not about our own worthiness, but rather His presence in us. Our worth and identity are placed squarely in Jesus, and His saving work on our behalf. We'll talk more about that in later chapters, as part of this section.

But for now, let's agree to this: production-as-worth is what the world around us reinforces daily, even hourly. Perhaps the most difficult work of a season with less output is learning to rest in the present, without needing to show anything for it. Perhaps what we need most is permission to stop trying so hard to create a full calendar or the next project, when nothing seems to be working toward that end.

I've been working on granting myself permission to rest for quite some time. Here's my journal entry from just ninety days into a very downsized life:

> *CHRISTY—GET THIS THROUGH YOUR THICK HEAD. IT'S OKAY NOT TO PRODUCE RIGHT NOW. IT'S OKAY NOT TO SPIT OUT PROFOUND IDEAS, LINES OF POETRY, DEEP SERMONS, A BRANDED WEBSITE OF OFFERINGS. ALL OF THIS: REST, RECEIVING, TRUSTING, NOT FORCING—IT'S OKAY. IN FACT, IT IS RIGHT. YOU'RE OVERDRAWN; YOU'VE OVERSPENT YOURSELF. DON'T EXPECT THE ACCOUNT TO OVERFLOW ABUNDANTLY RIGHT AWAY. SLOW YOUR ROLL.*

(In case you are wondering, the answer is yes—I always abound in grace toward myself in this manner, especially while journaling.)

So while I was struggling one particular morning with feelings of angst about long, empty days and a fully available calendar, I phoned my friend Laura. Actually, she is more of a prophetic prayer-warrior, and sometimes we just need to talk with someone like this.

After she prayed a very powerful prayer over my falling-apartness, I poured out a bunch of words that felt completely inadequate to the disorientation that was now marking my days. Laura paused, then responded, "Wow. God's got you in a real 'Re' season, doesn't He?"

I let her words sink into my soul, and I turned them over to check them out from every angle. A real "Re" season, indeed.

"Re" seasons and Perspective

Isn't it interesting how just two letters—*re*—can remake a word? Mirriam-Webster points out that this prefix *re* can mark both forward and backward motion:

```
re- (prefix)
definition of re- (entry 4 of 4)
1: again : anew
retell
2: back : backward
recall  1
```

There are so many *re* words. Here are just a few:

renewal
restoration

reorientation
redemption
reworking
receiving
rethinking
repurposing
rebuilding

I could keep going, but I think we can see this truth: *re* words all seem to point inward first. It's like this: the work begins with me, and it must happen in me before anything else happens through me. How humbling, really. But a "Re" season also means God isn't done. And, again I say, how humbling, really.

My sweet friend Laura then said, "I sense the Lord saying that the fields need to remain fallow for a season, Christy." It was a real mic-drop moment for me, a moment of significance that brings about a new perspective to move forward well. Maybe a deeper understanding of the fallow field will help you in this season, too. In fact, it might just free you up in ways you didn't anticipate.

Understanding the Fallow Field

Fallow is not a word with which people today typically have familiarity, unless maybe they live on a farm, study agriculture, or they've been to seminary. I know, because I've been asking smart people, those whose vocabulary certainly exceeds mine, and they give me a confused look.

So here's what it means: A fallow field is one that is left plowed, but not sown with seeds, for at least one season. Farmers do this to help the ground recover, and to increase its fertility. For a whole season, they let the ground rest.

Farmers still make use of this fallow field method today. The fallow field isn't a new farming concept, though. It is ancient and biblical, in fact, which is why seminarians know something about it. In the Old Testament, the Israelites were instructed to let the ground lie fallow every seventh year. We can think of it sort of like a Sabbath for the soil—every seventh year, the ground was plowed but not planted.

You may wonder, then, how did the Israelites live without producing crops for an entire year? Good question! They were instructed to live off what the land produced *naturally* that year, and those who planned well may have squirreled away some resources from prior harvests to tide them over. So, in a significant act of obedience, every seventh year, the people released the ground from the expectation of production for an entire year.

In farming, I'm sure this concept makes a lot of sense. It's proven out in the healthy, substantial produce that follows. But in our daily lives, fallowness can be incredibly disorienting. It is countercultural to have a figurative field that doesn't yield crops in an age that celebrates all forms of heightened productivity. *Not* sewing seed in an empty field feels almost un-American, doesn't it? I mean, we live in the land of opportunity! How dare we let that ground lie without asking it to bring forth something meaningful? That sort of non-expectant farming in the field of life might even be deemed as putting good soil to waste.

And yet, the fallow field is biblical. Letting a field rest is about two things. In agriculture, the focus of a fallow field is the promise of far greater yield in the years to come. And in Scripture? The fallow field serves as a reminder of the "divine ownership and divine gift" of the land for God's people.[2]

Fallowness was a monumental reminder for the Israelites that they were working and producing from land that belonged not to them, but to God, and that God was also the one bringing everything that came from it. In a very base sort of way, the call to leave a field fallow every seventh year was about stewardship and obedience, much more than agriculture and soil structure.

In the same way that the Sabbath functioned for God's people, where six days of work yielded seven days of necessary functions for life, so the fallow field meant that six years of planting could accomplish seven years of supply. This very idea requires a great deal of trust. To live this would require God's people to skip the basic function of planting, deferring to God's plan of fallowness, which would be an act of obedience-in-faith, where the resulting provision would follow.

When Obedience Precedes Understanding

As we mature spiritually, there are times in each person's life where the opportunity to be obedient will come without complete understanding. Sometimes, there is not even partial understanding when our hearts are moved toward an act of obedience. We don't know why we feel so strongly prompted in a direction, but we can no longer deny that prompting. In our humanness, we'd like to understand what we're being asked to do, every time, before we do it. I think about my teens, and the

most common question they ask me. The question that most
frequents my time with them is, "Why?"

"Why can't I?" "Why should I?" "Why would you ask me to
do that?" Why is a question about understanding, but also
a natural question as we are seeking to keep building trust.
The heart of the why question is this: Let me understand your
motive!

Spiritually, the question of why is a place in which we can get
stuck. This is because we rarely, if ever, can understand God's
motives. His ways are higher than our ways; His thoughts are
higher than our thoughts.[3] If we had the mind of God, we
wouldn't be dependent on God at all, would we? But, alas—or
thankfully, depending on your perspective—we do *not* have the
mind of God.

We have a much smaller, human mind. It can be tempting
to flatten out the gospel, or to overlook the mystery of God.
But this would be a mistake! The hiddenness of God is our
starting point, and this is not something to lament, but rather
something to embrace. The altogether over-and-aboveness of
God makes Him worthy of our worship. If we could fully
understand God, would worshiping even make sense? We
worship God *precisely* because He is far greater than we, and
worthy of our praise.

As we seek to continue in trust, we frequently ask God the *why*
question in order to attempt to understand His motive. Here's
the thing, though: I know no one, in several decades of walking
alongside people in deep spiritual places, who would tell you
they have heard a clear answer to the question why?

Everyone comes to a place of asking the why question when they face hardship or trial. So many people get stuck here. We can offer this question up to God; He can handle all of our questions! In fact, I'd even venture to say He expects this question. We just need to release our hold on any sort of answer.

Let me offer an alternative way of connecting with God in seasons like these: consider asking questions that begin instead with *what*. What are you teaching me in this season, God? What do I need to pick up, and what do I need to let go of? What are you seeking to do in and through me? What requires more focus in my life? What redirection are you offering me in this turbulent time?

The questions that begin with what offer us the opportunity to move forward spiritually. These are trust-building questions, but rather than seeking motive for prior action, they point toward how God is moving in the current moment. I encourage you to journal on some of these questions and experience the unique freedom and hope that they can bring as you talk honestly with God.

When Signs Follow Obedience

While we often pray for signs that will show us which way to go or what to do in advance of the act of obedience, so we can walk into that with assurance, God more often operates the opposite way. God gives us a place for obedience, and the signs that we've chosen well tend to follow the sacrifice of the moment. The sooner we understand this, the easier it becomes to practice radical obedience, or even the small obedience of daily life.

I experienced this in a very powerful way when I was in seminary. Tuition was due for the next semester, but my funds were running short by over a thousand dollars. That was a big sum of money for me, and I didn't see the solution—but I did feel confident that God had called me to continue in seminary. So, I signed up for the next round of classes, knowing full-well I was short.

What came next was nothing short of dramatic. The week that payment was due for classes, I checked the mailbox and found a letter from a group in Florida, where I'd reached out about a scholarship opportunity. We'd exchanged an email, but the application they provided was actually a corrupt file, so I was unable to open it. In the busyness of life, I lost track of that opportunity.

I felt certain this letter was simply a courtesy; they were reaching out to let me know that, since I'd never actually applied, they were unable to provide support. Imagine my surprise when I tore open the envelope and a check fluttered out and fell to the driveway! I remember this as though it were yesterday; I stooped down to pick up the check and let out an exclamatory shout: they'd sent $1250. It was exactly the amount I needed to be whole, financially, for the classes.

The short letter they included simply said that they hoped this would release the financial pressure from my shoulders and allow me to continue in my study. I was overcome with gratitude.

If we were sharing coffee, I could tell you story upon story about situations like this: God's repeated provision in both small and very big ways when I stepped out in obedience. What

I would tell you, if I could look into your eyes and take hold of your hand, is that being obedient is always worth the risk, and that if you're waiting on some sort of sign to take the next step: Don't. Don't wait. Take the step. Signs so often follow, friend. Don't delay obedience for your own sense of understanding, or for some sort of sign that you're moving the right direction. Trust what God is saying to you, and move on it.

Trusting God with a Fallow Field

No one lets a field lie fallow without some twinge of missed opportunity. We come to the place of fallowness in multiple ways: some of us are nudged toward less productivity in a season, and so we pull back from the activities of planting, or we leave a job, or step back from an opportunity. This is a difficult way into fallowness! The other way is equally difficult; sometimes we find ourselves in a season like this without having chosen it. It almost seems that the fallowness has found us: opportunities dwindle, activity wanes, and we are left with an emptiness and a much more open calendar.

Shred-It Day

The days have dwindled to
nothingness
Long stretches with no
commitments
Except for the community

bank's "Shred-It Day" this
Thursday
Which I added to the
calendar a month ago
This must be a stripping
away
The place where I lay bare
No "to-do's," not one "yes,
done"
But just the empty day ahead
With nothing to do, but to be
So disorienting to me.
Lord, please help.

Maybe fallowness for you is less about activity level, and more about what you sense to be the level of productiveness in your life. Perhaps you aren't sensing the sort of fruit you once knew, or the level of fruit you feel you should be putting out. In seasons like this, it is particularly important to put focus on the soil over the seed and fruit.

Shifting Focus

There are two parts in the spiritual life: ours and God's. I've come to believe over time that I cannot do God's part, and that God will not do my part. When my part and God's part come together, the resulting force can be called "dual agency."

Agency is a relatively academic word for the capacity to bring about results, to impact change in life, and to keep moving forward. Each of us has agency in life, and we are exhibiting it at various levels: some of us have very high agency. You'll recognize a person with high agency because they can get things done, move the ball forward, and always seem to be accomplishing. Others of us have lower agency, particularly in tough seasons. With less agency, an individual seems to accomplish less, having a decreased impact overall. When agency is very low, we may feel overwhelmed by life. It is as though we are spinning out of control, and cannot seem to stop. Recognizing the level of agency we feel at any given time is an important part of self-awareness.

Just as we have been given agency by God, God also has tremendous agency in the world. His agency is always high! He can impact and do anything! Scripture tells us so. There are no limits to God's agency in the world, except those that He has given Himself in allowing us free will.

Our part then, spiritually, is ready ground; God is seeding, fertilizing, watering, and bringing growth from the soil of our hearts. This is His part.But trusting God when nothing seems to be forthcoming in your life is a real act of faith. Believing that God is not done when the field is lying fallow, but rather choosing to claim that He is purposefully allowing rest and preparation in your life, is a defiance of worldly wisdom. It is placing the truth about who we know God to be above the circumstances we can see. This sort of faith is especially necessary in seasons of fallowness.

Re-evaluating Busyness

Here's a question to sit with for a while: Have you ever felt very busy, but realized upon contemplation that you weren't in fact that fruitful? Because here's the truth: busy and fruitful aren't always related. *Sometimes, our busiest seasons are actually times when we aren't bearing a lot of fruit.*

Yikes. That idea of busy days with little to no fruit steps on my toes—and my to-dos—and my quest for a full calendar page. Maybe producing is more of a temptation for validation (from both ourselves and others) than many of us realize. Leaving fallow ground to rest is, rather counterintuitively, straight up hard work.

So, I full-on resisted these words from my friend Laura about letting the ground lie fallow. But my prophetic friend persisted: "God is giving you a break! Give yourself permission to rest. The work is internal, and spiritual," she insisted, "and if you attend to it well, it sets you up for success in the next season."

I knew Laura was right, even though it was tough to hear. I sometimes get consumed with what God wants to do *through* me, without considering that there is unfinished business to be done *in* me. And I believe I'm not alone.

Word Study

I love it when a word study in Scripture helps me grasp a concept or learn something new, and I learned something new about the passage where God calls the Israelites to let the field lie fallow. Don't worry, this quick Hebrew word study is amazingly simple, which is why I also found it incredibly profound.

Translators have a very hard job, really. Sometimes, there is not a word in the language they are translating to that matches the word they are translating from. For instance, in Exodus 23:11, the word that is translated into English as "lie fallow" actually means *to leave, forsake, permit*. It literally means, "you shall leave/forsake" [the land]. This passage also gets translated to "let it rest." As a Smith & Helwys commentary informed me, "'Let it rest' literally means 'let it drop.'"[4] That's right—drop it. Don't do it. Let it be.

It's not just that you *don't* plant the field; it's the attitude that you *won't* plant the field. The Israelites weren't just *accepting* a field that was plowed but not sown, they were *embracing* that unsown field.

This brought to mind a word study I did years ago on the classic and often-quoted passage of Scripture found in Psalm 46:10, "Be still and know that I am God." In a very difficult pregnancy season, this verse kept showing up for me, as though it were chasing my life. Whenever a passage of Scripture comes around more than twice, I feel the need to explore it: what might the Spirit be saying to me through this passage?

As I dug into the phrase "be still," I was surprised to learn that it could also be faithfully translated, "hang limp" or "let it go."[5] It's an important distinction to me, because I can definitely be still while also continuing to cling to something. But the exhortation to let it go or to hang limp—these mean something different to me. These inform my heart and my spiritual posture.

It is much the same for the concept of fallowness. "Let it drop" tells my heart that I can release the need for productivity in a season and trust God completely to accomplish what is best in the field of my life. It also tells my heart that I can stop apologizing for this unplanted season and lean into the mystery of it, simply because God has allowed it. I don't have to try to figure out how to plant the field myself! Actually, I need to come to the place where I *won't* try to figure out how to plant the field myself. I can let it drop—and that is not only okay, it is right.

When God's Work Is Not Visible to Us

Scripture tells us that God never sleeps and never slumbers. God is always working, and there are moments we get to glimpse His activity in or through us, or the ways at which He is at work in the world around us.

Here's the thing I'm finding: those moments where we know exactly where God is at work in us or through us, or in the world around us, even—those are not the predominant stuff of life! More often, God's work is hidden, it seems; the soil has been tilled and something is happening underground that we can't see or name on the surface. This work is mysterious, buried deep in our souls. It is a work of waiting in our hearts and minds; active expectancy that is building. The ground is becoming pregnant with possibility.

Hidden work can feel frustrating. Is anything really happening in the soil of my life, you may wonder? What if the primary work in a season of fallowness is actually a massive reorientation of our heart toward God's ownership and provision in our lives? Might that be one part of what He is doing in us, as He allows us to experience time without visible production?

For me, yielding to the days of doing less and learning to own the work that is happening in the deeper spaces of my heart has been what obedience looks like. And now, as I write these words, this is evidence that the signs follow obedience: this book is the very real fruit of a fallow season in my spiritual life. But coming to this place was not easy, nor do I think it ever is easy to move through a period of time where there's not a lot to point to, when it comes to getting things done and building something people can see and admire.

Exactly one week after my self-talk smackdown and the declaration to slow my roll, my journal entry reads like this:

"BE BRAVE. BE STRONG. DON'T GIVE UP. EXPECT GOD TO GET HERE SOON." (PS. 31:24)

I FEEL LIKE I NEED THIS AS A TATTOO—OR TO PUT IT ALL OVER MY HOME—SO I READ IT EVERY DAY. LORD, I KNOW YOU ARE COMING. I SENSE IT IN MY BEING; MY HEART QUICKENS AS I THINK ABOUT HOW YOU ARE ON YOUR WAY.

REDEEM, RESTORE. THOSE ARE TWO WORDS I FELT YOU GAVE ME WHEN THE FIELDS WENT FALLOW. NOW I'M THINKING ABOUT LAZARUS—AND HOW, WITH HUMAN EYES, IT SEEMED YOU WERE TOO LATE. BUT, WE HUMANS FORGET THAT YOU ARE NOT BOUND TO OUR RULES, OUR TIMETABLE. SO, I'M ASKING YOU TO

COME QUICKLY, SO YOU DON'T HAVE TO RESURRECT, BECAUSE I'M NOT CERTAIN MY HEART CAN TAKE FULL ON DEATH, THE TOMB AND THE STENCH.

IN MY HEART, I HEAR YOUR WORDS: "DID I NOT TELL YOU THAT IF YOU BELIEVED, YOU WOULD SEE THE GLORY OF GOD?"

OH LORD! I WANT SO MUCH TO BELIEVE LIKE THAT. I ASK YOU TO PLEASE HELP MY UNBELIEF. MAKE ME ABLE TO STAND STRONG IN YOU; SET MY FEET ON YOUR WORD, AND MY FACE LIKE FLINT TOWARD YOUR WAYS. AMEN.

Help my unbelief. Make me able to stand strong in You. This is God's work in me right now, in this season. Maybe this is also what God is doing in you during this time of fallow ground.

The Hidden Work

I'm longing to see the hidden
work:
the places You are moving
me
toward a better depiction of
Your glory
I'm longing to feel the

hidden work:
holy unrest in the deepest
parts,
crisp purpose, fresh faith in
this stale heart
I'm longing to hear the
hidden work:
pure songs and melodies,
authentic new rhythms
birthed in me
I'm longing to taste the
hidden work:
like manna and quail,
raining down,
daily provision mysteriously
gathered from underground
I'm longing to know the
hidden work,
but all that is happening
where the roots grow
must be spoken in faith
before it's recognized and
known
Until the hidden work
surfaces, by Your grace,
help me to hope solely in You
and continue to seek Your
face.

1. https://www.merriam-webster.com/dictionary/re/.

2. David Noel Freedman, ed., Anchor Bible Dictionary, vol. 3, H–J (New York: Doubleday, 1992), 1026.

3. See Isaiah 55:8-9.

4. William Johnstone, Exodus 20–40, Smith & Helwys Bible Commentary(Macon, GA: Smith & Helwys, 2014), 174.

5. Robert L. Thomas, NAS Exhaustive Concordance of the Bible with Hebrew-Aramaic and Greek Dictionaries (Nashville: Holman Bible Publishers, 1981).

11

— • —

THEN, THERE'S JUBILEE

Jubilee

Just when it's too late to
plant,
when the heat is descending
and the window for
originating
kernels of possibility
underground has closed;
Just when you start to count
the cost
of letting this ground rest
by remembering what won't
be coming forth,
what won't be breaking
through the soil this season;
Just when you are sure you
should have
spilled out that one packet of
seed,

the ninety-nine cent variety
you stashed away
years ago for a season like
this,
but somehow forgot between
the busyness of the day
and the never-ending
nothingness of the now;
Just then, there is a burst of
green!
Epiphany—a stunning
revelation
birthed quietly from
something buried within,
without your help, sans seed.
Maybe the best things are
happening
deep in the dirt of our souls
where we have no business
trying to control
outcomes, varieties, species,
product,
But rather, the gift might be
whatever makes its way
forward from the fallow,
just when you were sure
nothing was coming.
These wild surprises have a
name;
We call these untamed gains
Jubilee.

I love the way Jesus introduces his ministry in Luke 4. Picture the thirty-year-old standing in the temple, about to read. He's handed a scroll of the book of Isaiah, and he unrolls it to Isaiah 61. Here are the words he reads:

> The spirit of the Lord God is upon me,
> because the Lord has anointed me;
> he has sent me to bring good news to the
> oppressed,
> to bind up the brokenhearted,
> to proclaim liberty to the captives,
> and release to the prisoners;
> to proclaim the year of the Lord's favor,
> and the day of vengeance of our God;
> to comfort all who mourn;
> to provide for those who mourn in Zion—
> to give them a garland instead of ashes,
> the oil of gladness instead of mourning,
> the mantle of praise instead of a faint spirit.
> (Isa. 61:1-3, NRSV)

In the message, it is translated like this:

> He came to Nazareth where he had been raised.
> As he always did on the Sabbath, he went to the
> meeting place. When he stood up to read, he was

handed the scroll of the prophet Isaiah. Unrolling
the scroll, he found the place where it was written,

God's Spirit is on me;
he's chosen me to preach the Message of good
news to the poor,
Sent me to announce pardon to prisoners and
recovery of sight to the blind,
To set the burdened and battered free,
to announce, "This is God's time to shine!"

He rolled up the scroll, handed it back to the
assistant, and sat down. Every eye in the place was
on him, intent. Then he started in, "You've just
heard Scripture make history. It came true just
now in this place." (Luke 4:16-19)

Jesus is boldly announcing the inbreaking Kingdom of God.
Eugene Peterson has translated it brilliantly: This is God's
time to shine! Jesus is telling all those gathered in the temple,
I'm here to do the things that have been prophesied: look no
further. I am the fulfillment of this promise.

It's a big, huge promise that Jesus is referencing. He's talking
about the restorative plan of God, painting in large but
masterful strokes the way He is now on the scene to fulfill
these promises. Jesus is bringing good news and comfort. He's
releasing those who are bound up, and those who are captive.
He's mending broken hearts and bringing gladness where
there has been great pain. These are words to revel in, and to
celebrate.

This is also what the Kingdom of God is all about! Those who heard these words in real time from Jesus's lips unfortunately interpreted the words all wrong: they were looking for an earthly kingdom that would set things right, overthrow the oppressive Roman government, and restore some of the tangible things that had been lost, as well as the intangible dignity of the Israelites as they lived under the thumb of Roman oppression. This is why the people laid palms at the feet of Jesus when he entered Jerusalem. They were hailing him as an earthly king, because they could imagine nothing better or more paramount to change their condition.

We are so often just like those who walked with Jesus more than two centuries ago. Our finite minds cannot imagine a better way for Jesus to bring restoration and justice than for there to be change right here, right now, in the systems and structures in which we live, and this is not altogether a wrong or ill-placed idea. We should absolutely long for justice in the here and now, as Christ-followers, and do everything we can to bring it about.

However, Jesus was not establishing an earthly kingdom, but rather a heavenly Kingdom. His Kingdom would not be temporary, in an earthly sort of way. His Kingdom would be eternal, it would never end. And Jesus's way of setting things right for all of us favors the long game of eternity and the permanence of neverending life, although we begin to flesh it out right here, on earth, as we walk with Him right now.

Understanding Jubilee

In the twenty-fifth chapter of Leviticus, we are introduced to something called Jubilee, which happens only twice a century in biblical times. It's pretty unique. In fact, some commentators have wondered if it was too idealistic and utopian to be actually lived out, although with certainty it was commanded by God of the Israelites.

Every fiftieth year, according to Leviticus, something really special happened: that was the year of release or liberty, also called Jubilee. What I'm about to say is difficult to believe, but it is exactly what Scripture tells us. For Israelites in the Jubilee year, all debts were canceled, and the people would return any homes or property to the original owner. You read that right! Whatever debts people owed one another, if they were Israelites, were canceled completely—no longer owed.

Take a moment to let that sink in. So, imagine what it would be like if, every fifty years, we no longer owed a mortgage or student loans (Can I get an Amen?), and if we'd borrowed from a neighbor–that balance would be wiped away, too. Sounds unbelievable, right? But it's a part of the Old Testament practice, according to Leviticus.

In this way, equality was restored to the Israelites in property ownership, because everything reverted back to the original owner. And if an Israelite fell upon the hardest of times and was forced to sell themselves into bondage to another Israelite, in the year of Jubilee, they were released. What a year of freedom for so many!

Agriculturally, in the year of Jubilee, again there was again no sowing, reaping, or harvesting. Because the ground was left fallow every seventh year, year 49 was a fallow year. Jubilee meant that year 50 was a second, fallow year. Imagine the trust it must take for a people who, in many ways, relied on the land for their well-being and prosperity to let it rest and rely solely on God! Yet, the rhythm continued, every fiftieth year, as the people released one another from all debts, and property rights reverted to original owners.

God's people were not without a promise of provision, as they moved into Jubilee. In Leviticus 25:19-22, an abundant crop is promised in the year prior to the fallow year preceding Jubilee; in this way, its threefold abundance would meet the people's need through this season of forgoing the work of harvest.[1] Additionally, there is evidence of significant aftergrowth as promised, including "at times, two or three harvests" obtained from "one sowing in the Galilee highlands and in the Wadi Artas near Bethlehem."[2]

Jubilee was signaled every fiftieth year by a ram's horn, called the *sopar*, being blown, long and loud. Incidentally, the same sort of ram's horn was also often used in other ways, including as a call to muster an army, as the battle cry, to frighten the enemy, and to proclaim a victory.[3]

There are days I feel pretty desperate for a spiritual Jubilee. I long in the deepest places for things to be set right in my world, my family's world, and in the whole wide world. I long to be free from the things that seem to have a hold on my heart. In very real ways, my soul calls out for that fiftieth-year sort of experience.

And then, I remember: that's the work of the cross.

The forgiveness of our spiritual debts is accomplished in Christ's atoning work on the cross. Just as the ram's horn was sounded to begin Jubilee on the Day of Atonement, Christ's atoning work on the cross signals our release, or freedom, from

the weight of sin. I cannot underestimate the importance of
this connection in the life of a believer!

You see, it's no mistake that Jesus opened up the scroll of Isaiah
and found chapter 61; he was letting the listeners know that He
had come to bring a new kind of Jubilee. It's significant to note
that Jubilee was also sometimes called "the year of release"
or "the year of liberty."[4] Hear the language of Isaiah 61 once
more, knowing what you now know about Jubilee:

> The spirit of the Lord God is upon me,
> because the Lord has anointed me;
> he has sent me to bring good news to the
> oppressed,
> to bind up the brokenhearted,
> to proclaim *liberty to the captives,*
> and *release to the prisoners;*
> *to proclaim the year of the Lord's favor.*
> (Isa. 61:1-2a, NRSV; italics added)

This wouldn't be the limited, though freeing and righting,
experience of Jubilee as commanded of the Israelites in
Leviticus; rather, this would be a future state of freedom and
restoration that would span far beyond our day and time.

It is true that freedom is never really free. So this sort of
freedom came with the greatest cost. Jesus, once and for
all, bore all our debts on his shoulders and endured a cross,
dying and then rising again on the third day. His death and
resurrection makes abundant life possible for you and for me.
Maybe hope for you, right now, is just beginning to embrace

that truth as it comes to the places you most need resurrection and freedom in this moment, today.

Theologically, the Israelites observed Jubilee as an act of obedience, but also because, in the faith required to live out this sort of radical fiftieth year, the people would be reminded that God is the only one who could be their Provider. It also served as a reorientation for ownership of any kind: following the commandment to return property and even people to the original family, canceling debt of any sort, reminded the Israelites that God was ultimately the owner of it all and that they owned nothing but experienced daily God's gift of provision.

I've begun to ask the question, how has this season of limited production and fallowness contributed to new beginnings for me, relative to understanding God's gift of provision in my life? How have I been reminded in this season that I don't own anything, but rather I steward it all in this life? How has the loss of productivity allowed for new, highly necessary things to spring forth in my life?

This is a glimpse of the restoring work of Jubilee, and because God is unchanging and so faithful, we can know that what He intended to do for the Israelites He also intends to do for us. How might this season be a divine blessing in your life? What is the good that is growing now in your life that would never have been present if you'd been able to keep churning out the goods of whatever you've always planted?

If your fields are fallow, if your days are long and you don't have much fruit to show, if you are confident the ground has been tilled but you cannot find the seed packets anywhere, and it is far too late to put them in the ground now—then this is for you.

Rest, dear friend. Perhaps, this is a year of Jubilee in your life, where the redeeming and restoring work of Christ is happening in ways you can't yet see, but your soul tells you that this is so. There is great purpose in the fallow field, and especially in the second year of fallowness called Jubilee. Countercultural, yes. But also biblical.

Embrace a season with no expectation of production, and let the ground rest. Then, embrace whatever the soil of your soul yields in this season, and allow those unexpected gifts to be called your Jubilee.

The Good News of Jubilee

I am bound in so many
places,
so many spaces of captivity
deep within me—
What will they think?
What will they say?
Am I enough?
All of this weighs
immeasurably on my soul,
the never-ending quest for
some control.

So, when I read that
You came to proclaim liberty
and open prison doors
to set people free,
my heart pounds.
And I wonder:
Will I also be found
in this Good News of Jubilee?
Could You sound the horn,
here and now,
long and loud—for me?

---

1. Lloyd R. Bailey, Leviticus–Numbers, Smith & Helwys
   Bible Commentary(Macon, GA: Smith & Helwys, 2005),
   301.
2. Jacob Milgrom, Leviticus 23–27, Anchor Bible
   Commentary (New York: Doubleday, 2001), 2158.
3. Jacob Milgrom, Leviticus 23–27, 2164.
4. William Johnstone, Exodus 20–40, 176.

12

EXPECTANT WAITING

"I pray to God—my life a prayer—
and wait for what he'll say and do.
My life's on the line before God, my Lord,
waiting and watching till morning,
waiting and watching till morning."
(Ps 130:5-6)

Only Believe
(based on Mark 5:35-43)

When you're sure it's over
and done,
and the word is sent:
"Don't even bother
Jesus—death has surely
descended"
When the mourners gather,
shrouded in black, weeping

and tears,
and make light of hope,
mocking any chance at life—

MAKE ROOM FOR JESUS!

Clear out the house that
reeks of despair,
sweep aside fear, usher in
faith,
watch Jesus speak life.
What you once thought was
gone for good
now—somehow—only
sleeps.
Suspended between sunset
and sunrise
is the breath that now
returns
to the smallest, weakest
frame,
impossibility replaced with
awe.

We're left to contend with
two simple words:
"Only believe."

A decade or more ago, our family went tubing down a major river along with some friends. While a lot of time has passed, I still remember this trip vividly, because it was quite out of the ordinary. The brochure that caught our eye and drew us in for this experience said we'd take a lazy ride along the river that would last between sixty and ninety minutes. This sounded perfect for our crew of parents and kids with single-digit ages, not overly intense in experience or length of time.

We arrived early on a sunny, clear morning—seemingly perfect conditions for our river float. As the adventure expert helped us prepare for our ride down the river, we watched a series of mandatory videos about water safety, and what to do if our inner tube float flipped or if we were thrust into a downed tree, for instance. It sounded from these videos, which featured rushing water, rapids, and even people risking life and limb in one high-stakes water rescue, as if we might see some white water on this little tubing trip. I'll confess that my blood pressure was rising a bit as we watched the scenarios play out on the little DVD system in the riverside hut. Okay, yes: I'd already begun counting children's heads and figuring out which adult could manage how many kids, as we were clearly outnumbered that day on the water in a parent-to-kid ratio. However, the way this adventure was described and what we really experienced could not have been more different.

On the day we chose, the water levels were actually very, very low. The guide mentioned this, as he helped us climb onto our rafts in the water. He also gave us precise directions that seemed very important. We were told to watch for two kayaks, which we'd see hanging in the wooded tree line on our right as our adventure was winding down. The orange kayak would tell us we had just a quarter of a mile to go, so at that point we should start paddling toward the shoreline. Then a blue kayak would mark our exit point.

Our guide explained that we may need to "lift our bottoms a bit" to make it over some of the rocks, and that we might "move a bit slower" on this particular day. Apparently, the height of the river directly correlates with your speed in tubing. We were about to find this truth out, in no uncertain terms.

Three and a half hours later, we were still floating along at a pace that would not even register on a speedometer, I'm sure of it. We were hungry. Actually, we were hangry. We were thirsty, too, as we were woefully underprepared for this amount of time on the water. For nearly half a day, we'd been baking in the sun. Although we tried to make the best of it, with little kids in tow, we were beginning to wonder if our adventure would ever really come to an end.

The worst part was that, hours earlier, I had completely stopped enjoying the fabulous view of the majestic river and one-of-a-kind tree line and started squinting into the distance for any sign of kayaks. Orange, blue, anything hanging in the tree line would be cause for celebration—because it would mean we were coming to the end of this interminably long float along the river. Even in the midst of such a slow current, I never lost faith that we'd eventually find our way off of the water, and the hope that our endpoint was around the next bend kept me scanning the tree line for our exit. But the end was all I could focus on; surely we'd see those kayaks hanging in the tree line soon??

Defining Hope

Hope is a small word with big meaning that we don't often stop to define. We throw around the word hope a lot, in all sorts of circumstances:

Hope to see you soon!
I hope you'll find a way forward.
I hope I remembered to put the milk back in the fridge.
I hope I find lifelong love.
I hope I can make it through this day.
Hope you feel better soon.
I hope this road isn't still under construction.
I hope I get to travel somewhere exotic soon.
I hope I get a raise this year.
I hope I win the lottery.

Sometimes when we say we're hoping for something, we're really just wishing.

What's the difference between hoping and wishing? Well, wishing is the stuff of make-believe and Disney songs. Although wishing holds space for a possibility for something to happen, wishing is really different than hoping. Wishing is about a longshot; it's something we don't really expect to happen. It would be great if it did happen, but we're not holding our breath.

Maybe, with all this talk about wishing, you're hearing Jiminy Cricket swoon out the words, "When you wish upon a star, makes no difference where you are, anything your heart desires will come to you!" Now, try subbing in the word hope into this song. Doesn't take but a moment to see it doesn't work, because hope is fundamentally different.

Hope is about something we truly expect to happen, or something we believe can truly happen. While wishing feels improbable, hope is meant to be probable; we've already defined hope as an alert expectancy. Hope that is grounded in the promises and person of Christ does not disappoint! (Rom. 5:5 tells us that.)

But in a season where there are more questions than answers, hope can feel hard to come by. Maybe in the most difficult circumstances, wishing feels easier; the stakes are lower. We don't have to believe it can come to be in order to wish.

But hope, like faith, functions as a verb. Hope is an active choice to lean in toward who God says He is, what He promises, and what He has told us He is doing—whether we can see it or not.

Perhaps our frustration around finding hope in difficult times is compounded by the way we've misunderstood waiting.

Waiting Time Is Not Wasted Time

Most of us have a deeply held, internal belief: waiting time is wasted time. It's why we seek out the absolute shortest line in the grocery store, and why we grow impatient when individuals banter with the cashier instead of keeping the line moving. It's why we incessantly check our phones and our watches in any waiting room, and why we make reservations for dinner, so we don't have to wait! Our cultural distaste for waiting is why commodities now find their way to us overnight, or even same day, whether that is truly required or not: in a world that doesn't want to wait, being competitive as a marketer requires

that wait times are minimized. This is another subliminal
narrative that can impact our spiritual lives in profound ways.

In contrast to our worldly understanding of the negative
impact of waiting, repeatedly in the Bible, we are exhorted
to "wait on the Lord!" Why would we be repeatedly asked
throughout Scripture to do something that would be a waste?

Herein lies the big difference in how we've understood waiting:
waiting time doesn't seem to be wasted time in Scripture. In
fact, when it comes to key themes in Scripture, waiting seems
to be a pretty big deal, especially seen throughout the psalms:

> Wait on the Lord; be strong and take heart and
> wait for the LORD. (Ps. 27:14, NIV)

> Be still before the Lord, and wait patiently for
> him. (Ps. 37:7a, NIV)

> I wait for the Lord, my whole being waits, and in
> His word I put my hope. (Ps. 130:5, NIV)

> I waited patiently for the Lord, he turned to me
> and heard my cry. (Ps. 40:1, NIV)

There are so many more verses like this; the psalms are full of this language. Clearly waiting time is not always wasted time, especially biblically, but why is this true?

Two Kinds of Waiting in Spiritual Life

There are actually two ways to wait: we can wait passively or actively. The difference is not in the circumstances, but rather in our spiritual posture.

Waiting time that is productive spiritually is not passive time. Often, in situations where we are waiting on something, there is a great deal of spiritual work happening deep within us, but it is like underground work because others cannot see it.

In this way, waiting times are in fact *active* times of preparation. To understand this better, it helps to know that the word for "wait" in Scripture also often gets translated as "hope." Strong's Hebrew defines *qavah* as "to wait, look for, hope, or expect." Here are a few of those verses where translators have chosen the word "hope" over the word "wait":

> But those who hope the Lord will renew their strength. They will soar on wings like eagles; they will run and not grow weary, they will walk and not be faint. (Isa. 40:31, NIV)

> Guide me in your truth and teach me, for you are God my Savior, and my hope is in you all day long. (Ps. 25:5, NIV)

Substituting the word hope in place of wait helps me to think about this all differently, because hope isn't something that happens *to* us, but rather, something that we engage in. If you've faced a dark season before, you know that hope is something you must choose. Hope is an active word, not a passive word!

What Makes the Difference in Passive and Active Waiting?

Spiritually speaking, what we choose to elevate determines how we wait. When we elevate circumstances, we wait passively. This is because our focus is on what is happening *to* us; the situations of life that are overwhelming and difficult. It's easy to find ourselves here.

This is like my posture on the innertube, as I was floating nowhere fast. Laser-focused on the orange or blue kayak, I completely overlooked the joy of the ride. I knew the kayak was coming, but I allowed the act of waiting for the hanging vessel to overtake the moments on the river with my children and friends, and the amazing scenery and opportunity to do something really wonderful.

We do this spiritually, as well; all of us are waiting for something in life. Whether or not you're in a season that feels particularly heavy with a circumstantial wait, there is something in life that you're looking toward or hoping for; this is because our human hearts are geared toward the Kingdom of God, rather than the kingdom of this world. So we are always looking toward eternity and the hope of heaven. We are always living in the tension of the now-and-not-yet of the Kingdom, and that is a sort of waiting all unto itself.

Circumstantially, many of us are also in a time where we're waiting on a change of sea wind, so to speak: a new opportunity, a relational change, a better financial situation, or a medical miracle. So many things could be on this list! We wait passively when we elevate the thing we're waiting for, constantly scanning the horizon for the blue kayak that says we've arrived.

Here's the thing: passive waiting is not productive, spiritually. Passive waiting, which is grounded in what is happening *to* me, can produce some undesirable fruit: bitterness, despair, sadness, hopelessness. Also, when we are hyper-focused on outcomes or what we think needs to happen next in our lives, that can create another set of problems, when we try to make it happen on our own. "A grasping person stirs up trouble but trust in God brings a sense of well-being," the writer tells us in Proverbs 28:25.

A Better Way to Wait

Another way to wait takes a more active posture. Active waiting focuses beyond the circumstantial evidence, or what is happening *to* me, and instead asks, what is God's purpose *for* me and *in* me, in this season.

Maybe you've been in a science lab at some point in your life and experienced the different tools available when performing an experiment. A lot of lab work uses the microscope, which takes one cell or one section of cells and makes it larger than life to see its inner workings. What you put onto the cell slide of your life matters greatly. Rather than studying your circumstances, I'm inviting you to study what God has said, and how God may be at work in your current situation. Put that on the cell slide;

magnify it, study it. Keep returning to it while you wait, and you'll be waiting actively, rather than passively.

When we elevate God's purposes, and focus upon His work *in* us during this waiting time, the fruit changes! Rather than bitterness, we work with the Holy Spirit as our guide to process pain and experience healing. Rather than despair, we begin to be expectant, by God's power that is working in us. Sadness doesn't take center stage; it is replaced by joy that comes from knowing that God is, in fact, at work as He has promised. And rather than feeling hopeless, we are filled to overflowing with the resurrection power of Christ! Indeed, active waiting does not diminish us, rather it enlarges our souls for what comes next.

Active Waiting is Honest Waiting

Maybe you're thinking, I don't feel very hopeful right now. If that is what is running through your mind, I invite you to begin there with God. Here's a real-life journal entry from the height of a season of waiting in my life. I'd classify this entry as a very honest prayer, leaning toward God, and attempting to focus on hope.

EXPECTANT: I'M TRYING SO HARD TO FEEL THIS EMOTION. YESTERDAY, I SAW A CLIP WHERE A SOLDIER IN TRAINING JUMPED ONTO A HANGING ROPE AND CLIMBED IT EFFORTLESSLY, ARM OVER ARM, TO THE TOP. THAT USED TO BE ME, TOO—BUT NOT ANY MORE. NOW I FEEL LIKE THE ROPE IS HOPE, AND I'M JUST DANGLING ON THE END, TRYING NOT TO LOSE MY GRIP. MY HANDS ARE ROPE-BURNED FROM

TRYING TO CLIMB, LOSING MY GRIP, AND PERILOUSLY
SLIDING BACK DOWN. I NO LONGER SEEM TO HAVE THE
INTERNAL FORTITUDE FOR THAT ARM-OVER-ARM
ACTION—IT REQUIRES A LEVEL OR GEAR I CANNOT
SEEM TO ACCESS. LORD, MORE THAN ANYTHING
I WANT TO BELIEVE. PLEASE HELP MY UNBELIEF.
PLEASE. AMEN.

If you resonate with these words; if the rope is hope in your life, and you're just dangling on the end, trying not to lose your grip, I implore you to keep showing up. Fold those rope-burned hands in prayer, and keep offering your days to God.

Another example from my journal:

IN MANY WAYS, I FEEL LIKE A PLAYER WAITING TO BE
SENT INTO THE GAME. YOU'RE MAKING AND RUNNING
THE PLAYS, GOD. I FEEL READY, BUT YOU ALONE
KNOW THE RIGHT TIME. I CHOOSE TRUST. AMEN.

Many, many times my journal entry reads some version of this:

GOD, I KNOW YOU ARE DOING SOMETHING NEW. I
CONFESS THAT I DO NOT PERCEIVE IT. PLEASE HELP
ME TO STAY EXPECTANT. HELP ME NOT TO GIVE UP.

This is what active waiting looks like for me. My journal is filled with honest reflection on daily life, the highs and lows, the breakthroughs and the struggles, all the while striving to keep

God's work in my life on the microscope slide, rather than my circumstances. I don't always get it right, and I bet you won't, either. There is one thing, though, that I feel I have gotten right in this season of waiting, and I will boldly share it with you: "My journal is filled."

My Morning Liturgy

My journal is filled because, no matter what, I practice this rhythm, which has grounded me and has provided a life-giving anchor in turbulent days. Just last week, a younger ministry friend asked me what my spiritual rhythm looks like. We talk about how important time with God is, spiritually, but we rarely break down what happens during that time.

Emily P. Freeman, in her podcast *The Next Right Thing*, talked about her own spiritual practices as a morning liturgy.[1] Her word choice resonates with me. A liturgy is the ritual or script we use in worship. In seminary, I picked up the idea that liturgy is the work of the people, for the people. Freeman is connecting the corporate work of the people, for the people, in public worship with our private worship, which is something we cultivate for our own relationship with God.

Here, then, is my morning liturgy: I begin with a good cup of coffee. Even the act of pouring and holding the cup is central to my routine. Bringing that coffee to a chair in the sunroom of my home, I sit and begin my time. Typically, I read some Scripture and possibly a devotional book. As I write this, I'm working through a book I found in a free pile at the seminary library, and it is rich and wonderful. In other words, I use what I have; it's not a complicated search for the perfect book. As I stay attuned to this process, the right resources seem to find me.

As for Scripture, I've read according to a plan, and I've also freely picked and chosen sections of the Bible for a time. As you've probably noted in this chapter, I have a deep affinity for the psalms. However, last year I read through the whole of Scripture, using the translation of the Message, and it was a great time of growth, spiritually, in my life.

After I've spent some time mulling over a passage of Scripture, I move into reflection through writing and prayer. Most often, my journal entries take the form of a prayer; there is usually confession and definitely adoration of who God is. I spend time writing about where I'm struggling and also thanking God for the places I see Him at work. Every now and again, this takes the form of poetry, and when that happens, it is usually because the poetry has begun to write itself in my mind before I pick up the journal.

Some days, I write out a section of Scripture in my journal that has risen to the top. It may be a phrase or a verse. Of course, this is also where notecards come in! When a verse "settles on my soul," as my grandmother Kingrey would say, I am attentive to that, and place it on a notecard so I can have it close by and recall it quickly. (Even as I'm writing this book, I regularly carry around notecards. For instance, I included Prov. 28:25 in this chapter, and I did not need to look it up—I simply typed it from my notecard. That verse has been traveling with me over this season of active waiting, which is one reason I felt led to include it here for you.)

Only when this time is complete, do I feel ready for the day. It doesn't have to be an incredibly long time; in fact, it can be as short as fifteen or twenty minutes, but some days I spend more than an hour. I hold this time with an open hand, and I ask God to reveal Himself to me as I wait for Him. But, for my soul, this time is vital. Recently, on a vacation, my husband and I were talking about getting an early start for an excursion. I backed up the start time for my personal wake-up time to include this morning liturgy. My husband asked if I might do it at another time, this once.

My response? "I need this time to feel ready to start the day."

My younger self wouldn't have said this. Not everyone feels this way, and I recognize this. For me, showing up each morning (whether I was "feeling" it or not) became the throughline, and a part of my lifeline in some of the hardest terrain.

Active waiting requires a rhythm, and that rhythm builds the cadence of hope.

ele

**Hope for Dry Bones
(based on Ezek 37:1-10)**

I survey the field of dry bones
Recognition: I have also been
them
but today I'm speaking hope

from experience
over whatever seems so far
gone,
you could never dream
it would once again live, and
breathe:
There is nothing—not one
thing
beyond God's re-forming
reach
He summons wind from the
four corners
at just the right time
and He alone breathes life
over the driest of bones
the darkest of corners
and the hurt you carry so
deep.
Yes, He alone can help you
live again.

---

1. Emily P. Freeman, The Next Right Thing (podcast), episode 222.

13

RECLAIMING THE FIELD

The Great Rebuilder

God is on the scene
and the builders work faster
than the wreckers.
Quick hands recast bits and
pieces
into sturdy frames and
edifices.
Yes, now the demolition crew
admits defeat,
while the Great Rebuilder
never sleeps.
Reconstruction is afoot;
restoration is coming!
Just wait and see.
This I know with certainty:
No one who hopes in God
ever regrets it.

We've considered at length the parable of the sower, which is repeated in Matthew 13:1-23, Mark 4:1-20, and Luke 8:4-15. In the Gospel of Matthew, this parable is immediately followed by another parable Jesus tells, commonly called the parable of the tares, or the parable of the wheat and weeds:

> He told another story. "God's kingdom is like a farmer who planted good seed in his field. That night, while his hired men were asleep, his enemy sowed thistles all through the wheat and slipped away before dawn. When the first green shoots appeared and the grain began to form, the thistles showed up, too.
>
> "The farmhands came to the farmer and said, 'Master, that was clean seed you planted, wasn't it? Where did these thistles come from?'
>
> "He answered, 'Some enemy did this.'
>
> "The farmhands asked, 'Should we weed out the thistles?'
>
> "He said, 'No, if you weed the thistles, you'll pull up the wheat, too. Let them grow together until harvest time. Then I'll instruct the harvesters to pull up the thistles and tie them in bundles for the

fire, then gather the wheat and put it in the barn.'"
(Matt 13:24-30)

Very thankfully, Jesus also explains this parable:

> So he explained. "The farmer who sows the pure
> seed is the Son of Man. The field is the world,
> the pure seeds are subjects of the kingdom, the
> thistles are subjects of the Devil, and the enemy
> who sows them is the Devil. The harvest is the
> end of the age, the curtain of history. The harvest
> hands are angels.
>
> "The picture of thistles pulled up and burned is a
> scene from the final act. The Son of Man will send
> his angels, weed out the thistles from his kingdom,
> pitch them in the trash, and be done with them.
> They are going to complain to high heaven, but
> nobody is going to listen. At the same time, ripe,
> holy lives will mature and adorn the kingdom of
> their Father.
>
> "Are you listening to this? Really listening?"
> (Matt 13:37-43)

There Are Two Sowers

What strikes me about this second parable is the way that Jesus
introduces a second sower, whose intent is malicious and whose
target is the world. (This means, as a person in this world, you

are a target for this sower.) That sower, who Jesus names as the Devil, is our adversary, our absolute worst enemy.

An awareness of the second sower, who sows not for us but against us, is vital in every season, but especially in seasons of the fallow field. Shortly after reading this parable, I wrote this in my journal:

> I HEAR THE SPIRIT SAYING THAT THE ADVERSARY IS PLANTING THISTLES IN MY LIFE.
> GOD! PROTECT THIS GROUND! COVER THIS SOIL!
> ROOT UP THE ENEMY'S SOWING,
> IN MY LIFE AND IN THE LIFE OF MY FAMILY.
> FORGIVE MY UNBELIEF, GOD.
> SHOW ME WHAT TO DO.

How Do We Recognize Thistles, Tares, or Weeds?

In my experience, both time and prayer are necessary to reveal patterns of sowing that are not of Christ. For instance, in my own life, the adversary's work shows up most prevalently in three areas: discouragement, doubt, and despair.

Although I certainly recognize those feelings as they are happening in me, at the moment these feelings are bubbling up, I am not always quick to name the source. I sometimes have difficulty recognizing spiritual attack in the moment, but as I stay connected to Jesus, the realization surfaces that someone is at work against me, who is absolutely sowing in weeds in the soil of my heart.

Naming this sort of attack on the field of our hearts is essential, because the act of calling out the enemy's work enables us to know how to stand firm in Christ, against the tactics of our adversary. If this all sounds like serious business, it is! Scripture is clear on this:

> God is strong, and he wants you strong. So take everything the Master has set out for you, well-made weapons of the best materials. And put them to use so you will be able to stand up to everything the Devil throws your way. This is no weekend war that we'll walk away from and forget about in a couple of hours. This is for keeps, a life-or-death fight to the finish against the Devil and all his angels. (Eph 6:10-12)

The tricky part about Satan's sowing is twofold. First, in this parable, the weed isn't easily distinguishable when it first breaks through the ground from the actual wheat, or good seed. The word used for sowing in this parable is actually different from the word used in the prior parable of the Sower.

Here, Jesus uses the verb *espario*, which is "to sow after." This implies that Satan's seed is sown after the good seed and intermingles with it in the ground. Until its growth is near complete, the shoots look very similar.

Secondly, the enemy sneaks in and sows at night, while we sleep. If that sounds sinister, it is! Sleeping is a very real part of life, a necessary function! This means the enemy is sowing not while you're doing something you shouldn't, but rather while you are engaged in something you should be doing, which is rest. From this understanding, we can learn to expect the enemy to sow in weeds, as a regular practice, on our most ordinary days, while we are also going about the necessary parts of life.

So Much More the Fallow Field

If Satan sows an already sown field, let us not be foolish; how much more eager Satan must be to sow the fallow field! Remember, the fallow field is a field which has been tilled and lies empty. How attractive this sort of field must be to an enemy with handfuls of destructive seed! No quicker way to bring someone down than to fill their tilled field with weeds.

To Reclaim the Field, Check Your Lean

Oftentimes, when someone is struggling in life and they speak to me about it, I exhort them to "lean in to Jesus." There are really only two postures in faith life: leaning in and pushing away. Did you know you can only lean one way at a time? It's true; you can't lean in multiple directions. In seasons of struggle, we've got to be certain we are leaning wholly on Jesus, and His strength and power.

One part of humility in Christ is not leaning on your understanding, but rather on God. The writer of Ephesians goes on to describe this work of leaning in as part of spiritual life, and the words here are helpful in understanding how this leaning posture happens:

Be prepared. You're up against far more than you
can handle on your own. Take all the help you can
get, every weapon God has issued, so that when it's
all over but the shouting you'll still be on your feet.
Truth, righteousness, peace, faith, and salvation
are more than words. Learn how to apply them.
You'll need them throughout your life. God's
Word is an indispensable weapon. In the same way,
prayer is essential in this ongoing warfare. Pray
hard and long. Pray for your brothers and sisters.
Keep your eyes open. Keep each other's spirits
up so that no one falls behind or drops out. (Eph
6:13-18)

This verse offers a great insight: "Truth, righteousness, peace,
faith and salvation are more than words. Learn how to apply
them." So let's do just that.

Truth

In very real terms, there is an ongoing battle for your mind.
This is why the Bible talks about renewing our mind on a
daily basis. It's also the reason that God's Word is named "an
indispensable weapon" in this passage, because Scripture is full
of truth.

We consume a daily diet of words. Some of these words are
written, some are spoken. Often we don't even realize we're
consuming words, nor are we actively weighing their source.
But when we consume Scripture, we don't need to discern
whether or not the words will be true or helpful. Scripture is
always true and helpful!

While our enemy regularly whispers lies, sowing the seed of doubt, discouragement, and even despair, we must speak out truth. Where does the truth come from? Jesus says that He is the truth.[1] The more time we spend in His words and in His presence, the more grounded in truth we become.

Don't merely read the words of Scripture; become a consumer of the truth. In the same way you pack a snack for the day, bring a word or phrase from the Word that has spoken to your heart, and revisit it often. Consider making the truth you need to hear most into a breath prayer! Breathing in and out, make this a short phrase that you repeat. Here are two examples of breath prayers I've been using this week:

Breathing in: *Your power*
Breathing out: *moving through me*

Breathing in: *Guide me*
Breathing out: *Guard me*[2]

Think of truth not as one big meal in spiritual life that holds us over for a long time, like a banquet where we leave stuffed and don't even want to think about eating again, but rather like the frequent snack to which we turn any time we feel hunger pangs. Regularly turning toward a key thought in Scripture during the hours of the day will rewire your mind to nourish yourself with truth, and it will also help you to discern other voices more quickly, so that you might learn to root out any lies before they become seeded in your soul.

Righteousness

Righteousness is another word that is used often in religious circles but might feel difficult to define. So, here it is: a simple definition for righteousness. Righteousness is simply being right with God, and right with others. This is simple to understand, but not easy to do, because it requires a regular yielding of ourselves and a constant reorientation of our souls.

Application of righteousness, to borrow Peterson's phrase, might look like this: you feel a prompt about something you've said or done, and you seek to make it right. Or, as you reflect on your day, you recognize a place where you've fallen short, and you immediately bring it into the light of God's love, confessing it and receiving both forgiveness and power from the Spirit to move forward.

Again, righteousness becomes a very active word, as we seek to apply it in our lives. This is not something that describes us, but rather something that describes God. Through Christ, we are made righteous, not by our own work, but by His work on our behalf. To continually live in a place of applying righteousness, we must be willing to submit our lives wholly and make change as we feel prompted.

Peace

In spiritual life, we tend to think of peace as a feeling we strive to acquire. However, the peace that Scripture speaks of so often is also not in any way a passive sort of feeling. Peace, understood biblically, is not about the absence of conflict. Rather, it is about the abundant presence of Christ. So even in extreme difficulty, our souls may still know peace. Perhaps this is why Paul, in his letter to the church at Philippi, describes this peace as "passing all understanding." In our human selves, it makes no sense to feel peace when life is upside-down. But, in Christ, this sort of peace is possible. This proves out even more as we consider that Paul wrote about this peace from the inside of a prison cell!

Walking alongside those in difficulty, and also in turbulent times in my own life, I have absolutely experienced this peace. When looking at the circumstances, I would quickly admit that they were completely overwhelming. Yet somewhere deep within, I had a strong sense that all was well. That sense simply did not come from me; I didn't dream it up or speak it into being. The peace I'm describing came from walking closely with Jesus, and an abiding sense that whatever came next, He would be with me, and He would be working it for my good.[3]

I love the imagery that comes in next. From the prison cell, Paul tells us that this peace actually guards our hearts and minds in Christ Jesus. Think about that for a moment! When I consider the imagery of this verse, I envision little guards posted at my heart, protecting me from potential intruders who would disturb this peace. A guard is active, not passive. Think of this like your very own secret service detail, protecting your heart at every turn and helping you to stay the course, remembering that Christ is with you.

Faith and Salvation

Faith is not our work for God; rather, it is God's work in us. In other words, we can't drum up faith. We don't speak it into being. God's grace enables us to believe. Remember, God is always the Initiator; our response follows His call or His movement in our lives. Our part is to be receptive, and as we are willing to receive, God can increase our faith.

We see this in the earnest words spoke in Mark 9:24, "I believe, help my unbelief!" These words tumble out of the mouth of a father who is desperate for help for his son, who is demon-possessed. The father desperately wants to have faith, but realizes he lacks it in some ways. This beautiful prayer is one we can easily speak—and it is a prayer that I believe God honors and meets us in.

The opposite of faith is not doubt! We sometimes think that is so. Actually, the opposite of faith is self-reliance. To the extent we are able to recognize that we are not able to supply all of our own needs, this is the measure of faith we are able to have. There is only room for faith where we have decided that the work is beyond ourselves.

Here is where salvation happens: when we can admit that the work is so far beyond ourselves, we are unable to do it, and we can only be saved through Christ. It is a reliance on God and God alone that is voiced in a prayer of salvation: *God, I need You! Please do what I can't do. I'm giving my life to You, because I can't do it anymore, nor do I want to. I'm asking You to be in control.*

Operating from a place of faith and knowing the gift of salvation begins where our self-reliance ends. Oftentimes, the enemy's voice will whisper that God isn't really going to do the work, or that you cannot trust Him. Satan speaks these lies in an attempt to turn your focus back onto your own abilities or capacity in any situation. Root out that lie, and lean into these two truths instead: in Christ, all things are possible; and apart from God, you can do nothing.[4]

Coat Check

On occasion, I enjoy a nice night out, usually courtesy of my husband's job or professional affiliations. Often these nights include a coat check, and we hand over our outerwear to be stowed until we are ready to go. We typically receive a small sort of calling card bearing a number so the right coats can be returned to us on the flipside of the event.

I titled this chapter "Reclaiming the Field" with that coat check in mind. Specifically, I was inspired by Psalm 62. The psalmist writes about feeling ganged up on and overwhelmed by curses. In short, this is not an easy place to reside, and in the midst of this, the psalmist also writes about waiting. This specific refrain occurs twice in the relatively short psalm:

> God, the one and only—
> I'll wait as long as he says.
> Everything I need comes from him,
> so why not?
> He's solid rock under my feet,
> breathing room for my soul,
> An impregnable castle:
> I'm set for life. (Ps 62:1-2)

Notice that "check and reclaim" sort of action happening in this stanza? The psalmist "checks his coat" with confidence: *God, the one and only—I'll wait as long as he says.* The psalmist then immediately reclaims a promise, as though he is recalibrating his own heart: *Everything I need comes from him, so why not?*

This is what reclaiming the field looks like, in the simplest terms: *God, the one and only—I'll wait as long as You say. Everything I need comes from You, so why not?* This reclaiming work happens daily, hourly, even moment by moment as we walk with God. If you're searching for your claim ticket, you'll find everything you need in God's Word. With the psalmist, personalize the prayer and make it your own.

Here's a breath prayer in three parts, as you seek to reclaim the field today:

Breathing in: *You are*
Breathing out: *breathing room for my soul.*

Breathing in: *You are*
Breathing out: *an impregnable castle*

Breathing in: *I am*
Breathing out: *safe with You.*

Evicted

Hey, condemnation &
shame!
Your lease is OVERDUE.
The Landlord of this heart
is now evicting you.
You've been squatting far
too long

occupying my space
You settled where you don't
belong
inhabited my place
There's no rent you could
pay to stay
Another owns this property
You will never buy Him out:
He paid the utmost to set me
free.
So I'm posting this notice:
You have run out of time.
You've been the lousiest
tenants,
Now I'm taking back what's
mine.

---

1. John 14:6
2. Joyce Rupp, The Cup of Our Life: A Guide for Spiritual Growth (Notre Dame, IN: Ave Maria, 1997), 31, 34.
3. Romans 8:28
4. Matthew 19:26; John 15:5

14

Naming the New Growth

She Soars

The butterfly is a sage
beauty,
for the stuff of reinventing
may be the hardest work of
life.
Imagination to see a new way
forward,
the audacity to cocoon
oneself in order to attain it,
the ferocity to break out of
that self-made binding,
and the sheer risk of first
flight with newfound wings.
On the other side of
adversity,
she soars.

There's a lie that lurks in the shadows of less productivity. It creeps in when we least expect it; an unwanted visitor with a disheartening refrain: You don't matter. Maybe it's a little more cryptic and nuanced: You matter less when you produce less. But the lie ties together your worth and what you produce, in a tight corollary.

It couldn't be further from the truth, of course! You matter greatly. But we are incredibly susceptible to this lie in seasons where there is less to show from our existence, in the spaces where we are churning out fewer proofs of our insatiable productivity. While there isn't as much productivity on display in our lives, it is often true that a much deeper identity-oriented work is the hidden work that is happening deep in our souls. But the more months you move away from production, the harder that truth is to claim.

In my stack of notecards where I rehearse the truths my heart needs to remember, there is a card that says, "I AM ENOUGH RIGHT NOW." (I do know that all caps are the equivalent of shouting. Most often, this truth needs to be proclaimed like a shout to my soul, so I wrote it in this fashion to remember how loudly I need to speak it.)

The card goes on to say, "When external validation doesn't happen, internal valuation matters more than ever. I am valued beyond measure and eternally loved by Christ." This card comfortably stacks alongside cards filled with Scripture and I believe it belongs in that company. Although you won't find one reference in the Bible that translates exactly into the words above, you can rest in the fact this is one of the most deep-seated and profound truths that is laced through the whole of God's Word: You matter. You matter so much that Jesus gave His life for yours, friend.

You matter on the days you can point to a long list of items you've contributed to make this world a better place, and you matter—equally—on the days when you can't point to anything at all about what you're bringing into being. If you're moving mountains, or if you're sinking into pothole after pothole, you matter equally to God.

Sometimes, in seasons where we are producing very little or even nothing at all, it is tempting to think that we are unseen. Doesn't it feel that way? As though a world full of beautiful people continue to churn out the best stuff ever, their brilliance lighting up social media feeds everywhere? Like we are the only ones not putting something amazing into the world today? It can be a hard place to live, really. But if you are nodding your head and connecting with the idea of producing less, this chapter is especially for you.

Perhaps the most profound work of the Christian life is coming to a place of knowing this: God's love for us is not contingent on how we perform or what we do, but simply that we are His beloved. As this book draws to a close, I wondered this morning: Should this chapter be first? But I believe our hearts have needed the work that precedes this chapter in order to be able to enter more fully into how seen and known we actually are.

Knowing God through Experience

Throughout Scripture, God is named in two ways. First, God reveals Himself to His people by naming Himself:

I Am. (Ex. 3:13-15)

I am the LORD. (Isa. 42:8, but used from the beginning of Scripture)

Anytime you see the name, LORD, in all caps, the writer is not shouting! Rather, this is the way the writer is conveying the covenant name for God. Let the all-caps LORD remind you that God is unwavering in keeping His promises to us.

God's character is also revealed to people in the pages of Scripture who then boldly name God based on the ways that they have experienced Him. They offer new names as they come to know more of who God is and how He is working in their lives. Here are a few examples:

The Lord will Provide (Abraham, Gen. 22:14)
The Lord Our Healer (Moses, Ex. 15:26)
The Lord Our Banner (Moses, Ex. 17:15)
The Lord Our Peace (Gideon, Judg. 6:24)
The Lord My Shepherd (David, Ps. 23:1)
The Lord Our Righteous Savior (the prophet Jeremiah, Jer. 23:6)
The Lord is Here (the prophet Ezekiel, Ezek. 48:35)

Each of these names comes out of the way God has revealed Himself in a circumstance. But my favorite name of God that is given by an individual in Scripture is "the God who sees me." Hagar, the Egyptian slave of Sarah (Abraham's barren wife) gifts us with this very personal name for God, in a harrowing moment in the wilderness.

Genesis tells us the story: Hagar gives birth to Ishmael, who is Abraham's son, and then things get super-awkward with Sarah, the barren wife. By "super-awkward," I mean themes like jealousy, infertility as a badge of dishonor in this culture, and lots of tension, bragging, and even mocking that come next. It's ugly stuff that plays out on the pages of Scripture. Sarah is quite harsh with Hagar.

Years later, after Sarah finally gives birth to a son, tensions become unbearable. Hagar ends up fleeing with her then teenage son into the desert, at Abraham's behest. Circumstances have culminated in a deep division, and Hagar fears for her life. Although she has packed rations, the provisions run out, and she finds herself and her son far into the desert, with no food or water, and no place to go. She is just about to give up, to succumb to the brutal heat of the desert, when God speaks to her there and miraculously makes provision for Hagar and Ishmael. Out of her experience, she boldly names God: You are El Roi, the God who sees me.

This is a profound revelation and name for Hagar to speak. Hagar is not an Israelite, which puts her outside of the group who is traditionally blessed in the early pages of Scripture. She is also a slave, and a woman—two more strikes against her capacity to have agency. I sometimes ponder how hopeless things must have felt for Hagar, with responsibility for her son and herself and without any provision or a place to go. She was sure her life was ending; her desperation was authentic and I'm sure that, in her place, I would have felt desperate, too. And then, God moves—when she least expects it and most desperately needs Him.

When Our Agency is Low, God's Agency is Still High

There are times in life where our own sense of agency is low: we seem able to contribute less, or we have a decreased sense of control over outcomes. Perhaps we feel we're not functioning at the place of optimal outputs. Perhaps opportunity seems limited in a season. Maybe we've been sent away or have been excluded from what was our place of deep belonging. In these times, we may feel a lot like Hagar: we are desperate for change in our lives, but we feel we can't seem to make it happen. What do we do when it seems we're in circumstances we cannot change?

I have found it most helpful in seasons like this to set aside my sense of declining agency and place my focus instead on the limitless agency of God. This is one reason it is helpful to focus on the names of God, because it turns our hearts in very real ways toward His presence with us in all the places. It's important to note that the times that God is named may be mountaintop times, but God is named in these passages primarily for His presence alongside the person in a valley.

For instance, Gideon names God "The Lord Our Peace" on the heels of a massive invasion by the Midianites and directly following his own interaction with an angel. The name is given because he fears losing his life for having seen an angel face to face, but the Lord reassures him in the moment, "Peace be to you; do not fear, you shall not die." From this affirmation, Gideon names the Lord.

In Exodus 17, Moses names God "the Lord Our Banner." Here is another name I love! This name is given just following a fight with Amalek. It's a really important battle, where Moses is holding up a staff, and when his arms are extended up toward God, the Israelites are winning. Any time he lowers his arms, though, Amalek begins to win. Moses grows so tired in holding up his own arms that Aaron and Hur come alongside him and each hold up one of Moses's arms.

Ultimately, the Israelites win this major battle. Moses gives this name to God because the Lord is their rally cry, or the uniting force for the Israelites. His name is the flag the Israelites will fly: Moses is naming God as the central focus and the One to whom victory is owed.

Notice how, in each of the interactions above, the person naming God is the one who is experiencing low agency. Gideon names God when he is sure he will lose his life: this is the lowest point of agency we can experience, really. Moses names God after his people have experienced loss when they were fighting without God's protection, and they won the war only because of God's agency on their behalf. In both situations, the name of God arises from low agency on the part of the individual, and God's limitless agency on their behalf.

The same is true of Hagar. Hagar names God as "the God who sees me" after she has experienced this, due to her own incredibly low agency (three-times over, as an Egyptian, a slave, and a woman). God, in His awesomeness, sees Hagar! This changes everything. She names God out of the overwhelming gratitude that He has actually seen her and is helping her.

All this talk about naming God from our experience, particularly when we find ourselves in a desert place, or in a spot of low agency in life, where we feel we are losing ground, begs a question: How are you experiencing God right now in this season? If you were going to name God out of experience, what name would you assign?

This isn't a quick question, really. I'm asking you to think about where you've seen God's hand in this difficult time in your life. Where has He moved on your behalf? What is God actively teaching you? Here are a few examples that would be true in my own life:

The God Who Writes My Story
The Lord My Anchor
The God of Mysterious, Hidden Work
The God Who Carries Me
The Lord My Protector
The One Who Holds Me Together
The Lord Who Always Comes Through

Do you get the idea here? If those we read about in the Bible can name God from their experience, so can we. Make it real, and make it personal. Think about God's great agency on your behalf: how do you see His hand?

When We Receive New Names

Before my children were born, my husband and I spent hours naming them. Really, hours! We had a variety of name tests that were employed, including how the name sounded when spoken as a whole, the rhythmic nature of the name, the balance in the first, middle, and last name, and (my husband's addition) the shout test. If our child should ever have their name called out in a music venue or on a basketball court, for instance, could it be shouted well? You can see that we were serious about finding the right names for each child! No doubt, someone also put this sort of time and care into your name as well.

In Scripture, names are incredibly significant, as they also carry a meaning or promise for the life of that individual. For instance, Abram meant "exalted father." Later, God renamed Abram, giving him the name Abraham, or "father of a multitude." It's easy to see how this new name expanded on a promise, giving even more meaning for Abraham.

Another example is Simon, whose name means "he hears, obeys" and who is renamed Peter, meaning "stone." This becomes even more significant as Jesus declares, "and upon this rock I will build my church" (Matt. 16:18) Again, there is movement from hearing and obeying, to a foundational role in the early church, which is forever marked by Peter's new name.

One of my most meaningful experiences with God happened in 2002, as I was spending time in the Bible and praying about name changes in Scripture. The devotional I was reading implored me to pray this question, "God, if you were renaming me, what would my name be?"

A profound experience followed, which is carefully detailed in my journal, and led to my vocational calling in ministry and my work as an ordained pastor. I received four words while in prayer, which were impressed on my heart one at a time: blessed, daughter, anointed, and proclaimer.

The first two words were very much situational. That's because, in 2001, we lost my father very suddenly, while he was vacationing with my mom in Cape Cod. He went away and never came home, after suffering a massive stroke. It was an absolutely heartbreaking loss. My father was only 54, and as a young adult in my twenties, I began to walk a very hard road of grief.

As a result, the first word I heard, *blessed*, was especially difficult to hear. If you've come this far in this book, you know that I define blessedness as the nearness of God in any situation, not one set of circumstances that the world would point to as evidence of winning in life. In so many ways, 2001 was a year of great, great loss. There was no #winning to be seen, in worldly ways. We buried my father, and I struggled through a year of deep grief and depression.

But spiritually, God was revealing Himself to me as a Rebuilder and a Restorer. He was putting me back together, quite literally, when I felt like everything was falling apart. In this way, and because of His nearness, I was absolutely blessed.

The name *daughter* also stopped me in my tracks. I had been a daughter of my father, whom we'd lost; now God was reminding me that He is my eternal Father. Scripture tells us that God is "a father to the fatherless,"[1] and in many ways, I was beginning to experience Him in a paternal relationship I'd never known before.

The last two words, anointed and proclaimer, shaped my call in very clear ways. I began to understand that I'd been set apart for God's work in the world. A proclaimer is one who shares what God has done; I wanted to do nothing more.

That's my story, and I share it here because I am confident of this: God is also writing your story. What might He name you, today? I urge you to ask this question and keep holding it before God, asking Him to reveal to you what He sees in you. Some pieces of our identity in Christ are absolutely shared across all believers; other pieces are shaped by God's fingerprints on your life. He has unique plans for you, "good works which God has prepared in advance for us to do" (Eph 2:10).

There are times when my own sense of agency has been low when I've struggled to believe this idea that God has a specific plan for me and is working it out. That is so much easier to believe when great things are happening in me and through me! When it feels like I'm in a fallow season, and nothing is popping up, much less being planted, I struggle to see those good works that have been promised.

Here is a very important thing to know about fallow ground: fallow ground is still tended ground! It is tilled, and purposefully not sewn. The fallow field is not forgotten! Rather, a tilled and unsewn field is a sign of future possibility, a mark of great things to come. Understanding it this way is what enables us to move through the feeling of barrenness as those who are marked by intention and possibility. Every aspect of your existence is encompassed by God. You are seen

right now, in this moment, by the One who matters most, and
He is for you. Let that truth rise to the forefront as you move
through your day, and through all the days to come.

You see me

I'm drinking from the
"God-alive-sees-me-spring"
Where a woman on the run
named God from her
experience,
and I do believe You see me,
too.

---

1. Psalm 68:5

EPILOGUE

The Escape Room

How did I get here?
I rattle the doors and
windows,
but every one is locked.

Like an escape room for my
soul,
I'm unsure of where to go
what to work on first
to earn release
and it seems like time ticks
more loudly in this
shoebox-sized room
teeming with well disguised
clues.

So I raise a page of written

words:
Does this mean something?
Push on a table leg,
will this open a door?
My vexed mind gyrates
like a spinning top
will it ever stop?
And then I remember:
I can speak to You!
So I flail my arms in the air
a distress signal.
You see my two-armed
smoke flair
and You, who knit me
together
now begin unraveling the
threads
of confusion and
consternation
that comprise this ball of
stress.
And I confess:
I was hoping for clues!
But You—You know
what my soul needs most.
Turns out I need rest
more than answers to this
confounding holding space,
but in my quest to solve the
room
I kept missing Your grace.

I thought I was alone in here
walls closing in with doubt
and fear,
but You knew my
inbetweenness
needed to work out faith, and
rediscover hope.

Soon I'll do it,
Soon I'll be through it
and when the doors
open—sweet release!
You're here now, and also
waiting through the transom
for me.
So I can embrace this
mystery,
for when all I felt was stuck
You were at work setting me
free.

Those words: *Soon I'll do it, Soon I'll be through it.* I've
reread, repeated, and rehearsed those words for months and
months now, ever since I began writing this book. Am I
through it? I'm not sure. I'm coming to believe that we're never
through it, until we're with Jesus.

If you've come this far, my earnest prayer for you is that this book has somehow helped you to move forward, to make sense of things. I pray you've found comfort in its pages, and also grace, and yes—truth. (You knew that was coming, didn't you?)

Even today, I'm revisiting the soil of my own heart, asking where the rocks and weeds are, and if there is hard ground. It's daily work, even as I put the finishing touches on this manuscript. And today, my fiddle leaf fig tree continues to bud and spring forth new life—and each time that happens, I give thanks. I feel as though I'm growing right along with her.

Yes, I wrote a book. But I'm still not producing in all the ways I used to; maybe I won't do that again. Either way, I'm at peace, knowing that the God of the Universe has good works prepared, just for me—and I believe I'm doing them.

I pray that you come to this place of peace, as well, friend. And now, as you go—a blessing, because that's what pastors like me are prone to do. Receive this benediction, this good word, and let it soak into your soul:

A Benediction

As you go from here:
May the force be with you—
the overwhelming force of
God's presence and love!

May it embrace you when
you need it most,
envelop you when you're at

your end,
and surprise you when you
least expect it.

May this force take up
residence in your heart and
mind
and carry you, like a
power-full current,
into God's best in every
aspect of your being.

As you stay in step with the
Spirit,
may you rest in God's great
plan for your life,
whatever is next.

READING YOUR BIBLE

Approaches to Reading Scripture in a Regular Cadence

The Gospels – Just beginning to read the Bible? Starting with Matthew, Mark, Luke or John enables the reader to learn quickly about the life of Jesus, His key teachings, and miracles. Each writer brings a different perspective, and any of the gospels is a great place to begin. Try a chapter a day, reading slowly, and picturing yourself in the stories.

Psalms – the Psalms are excellent prayers, especially when you're not sure what to pray.

Proverbs – a book of wisdom that conveniently has 31 chapters. I've enjoyed taking a chapter a day, and picking one proverb from the chapter I've read that I will then journal about, or focus on for the day.

Five chapters a day – this will move you through the whole of Scripture in about eight months. However, consider pairing some Old Testament chapters alongside one or two chapters from the New Testament, as this will help you to stay engaged and experience variety in what you're reading. (You'll thank me for this approach somewhere around Leviticus.)

Letters – the New Testament offers 21 letters, written primarily to early Christians by Apostles. These letters are very practical (try James!) and, as such, a great place to spend time in scripture.

Which Translation?

Translations of scripture can vary greatly, depending on how the translator is working. Some translations are word-for-word, meaning the English translation will have approximately one word for each word that was in the original language. Other times, a thought-for-thought approach is used, so that the translator is reading each thought and then putting it into the English language. The result is often more easily readable, as a word-for-word approach can get a little awkward at times.

There are many opinions about which translation of the Bible one should read. Here is mine: Read the one you understand the best, and want to keep reading. I personally read across numerous translations, and that has gotten easier with Bible reading apps like YouVersion. In the YouVersion app, which I highly recommend, it is easy to toggle between translations, and this is a great place to consider options and see what you find most readable.

Here are several you might consider:

New International Version (NIV) (a thought-for-thought translation)

New Living Translation (NLT) (a thought-for-thought translation)

The Message (a loose paraphrase, making it highly readable)

English Standard Version (ESV) (a word-for-word translation)

Christian Standard Bible (CSB) (a word-for-word translation)

New Revised Standard Version (NRSV) (a word-for-word translation)

Happy Reading!

www.ingramcontent.com/pod-product-compliance
Lightning Source LLC
Chambersburg PA
CBHW060251150626
46553CB00019BA/1584